MW00572629

"In a time of burnout after bu[n] like practical questions of leadersmp can sometimes come at all. In this book, Scott Thomas helps the reader frame a healthy life, Christlike leadership, church accountability, and gospel-rooted productivity. This is not a book of quick fixes or productivity hacks; we have enough of those. This book speaks first not to the week's calendar or to a life's résumé but to the soul of the leader. This book will come as good news to those who want to model healthy leadership that can last."

Russell Moore, Public Theologian and Director of The Public Theology Project, *Christianity Today*

"Scott Thomas does a wonderful job of giving us practical and biblical descriptions intended for those God called into leadership. Though many books have been written on Christian leadership, Thomas's book offers thorough insight on being a leader that comprehensively follows and leans on the beautiful example of Jesus."

Doug Logan Jr., President of Grimké Seminary and Dean of Grimké Urban; associate director of Acts 29; author of *On the Block: Developing a Biblical Picture for Missional Engagement*

"Drawn from over three decades of ministry, Coach Thomas supplies twelve principles, reminding us that souls formed by the gospel become leaders who finish the game. Leaders, if you want to run strong and last long, start training with *The Gospel Shaped Leader!*"

Dave Harvey, President of Great Commission Collective; author of *When Sinners Say I Do, Am I Called?*, and *The Plurality Principle*

"In a day of almost constant bullying, burnout, and moral demise, it is heartening to know that there is one volume to which I can always turn and direct others for guidance. The way Scott consistently tethers leadership principles to the truth of the gospel has led to a wonderfully helpful and hopeful book for those involved in local church life. Highly recommended!"

Sam Storms, Bridgeway Church, Oklahoma City, OK

"Scott Thomas understands the unique challenges of ministry and what prevents churches (and their leaders) from flourishing over the long haul. He teaches us how ministry flows from intimacy with God and directs us toward skills we often neglect—things like self-awareness, emotional intelligence, and relational intuition. Whatever ministry role you are in, this wonderful book will help you find pathways to long-term health and vitality. Get a copy for your staff and elders!"

Gavin Ortlund, Senior Pastor, First Baptist Church of Ojai; author of *Finding the Right Hills to Die On*

"I can't think of a more timely resource on authentic, Jesus-shaped leadership. Experienced and would-be pastors alike will find much here to encourage and help. We really need the lessons of this book in our churches today."

Sam Allberry, Pastor; apologist; author of *7 Myths about Singleness*

"Leaders must keep an eye on their own souls if they are to endure long, difficult seasons. Scott's book will help leaders embrace and embody these commands, so they might not only endure but enjoy leading in difficult seasons."

Brian Lowe, Lead Pastor, Exodus Church, Belmont, NC

"Too often, pastors labor and sacrifice without all the necessary tools they need to survive and thrive within the internal demands and emotional stressors of ministry life. This work from Scott Thomas is written in a way that is approachable, personable, readable, challenging, practical, and life-changing. I predict that many church leaders will keep their copy of this book within close reach as a source of comfort, guidance, healing, and hope."

John West, Licensed Professional Counselor; National Certified Counselor; lead author of *Emotional Intelligence for Religious Leaders*

"By paying attention to how we lead ourselves and the impact that we have on others, *The Gospel Shaped Leader* reminds us to see ourselves the same way God does: as his beloved children serving a heavenly Father who delights to use weak people to accomplish his mighty purposes."

Bob Osborne, Executive Director, Serge

"I have the privilege of serving alongside Scott in pastoral ministry, and I see him live the truths in this book and pour them into the lives of younger, less experienced ministers—like me—constantly. I am eager for other church leaders to benefit from his wisdom and faithful ministry through these pages. It will be a blessing to their souls and their ministries."

Barnabas Piper, Assistant Pastor at Immanuel Church Nashville; author of *Help My Unbelief, Pastor's Kid,* and *Hoping for Happiness*

"The mark of a great book is accessibility and depth—this book displays both. You will be encouraged and challenged from the wisdom of a mature pastor who has walked this path with others. I can't wait to reread this book and process the coaching questions!"

Mark Reynolds, Senior Strategic Advisor, Redeemer City to City

THE GOSPEL SHAPED LEADER

Leaning on Jesus to Shepherd His People

Acts 20:28.

Scott Thomas

New
Growth
Press

newgrowthpress.com

New Growth Press, Greensboro, NC 27404
newgrowthpress.com
Copyright © 2021 by Scott Thomas

All rights reserved. No part of this publication may be reproduced, stored in a retrieval system, or transmitted in any form by any means, electronic, mechanical, photocopy, recording, or otherwise, without the prior permission of the publisher, except as provided by USA copyright law.

All names for people used as examples in this book have been changed out of respect for their privacy.

Exponential is a growing movement of activists committed to the multiplication of healthy new churches. Exponential Resources spotlights actionable principles, ideas and solutions for the accelerated multiplication of healthy, reproducing faith communities. For more information, visit www.exponential.org

Unless otherwise indicated, Scripture quotations are taken from the ESV® Bible (The Holy Bible, English Standard Version®). ESV® Text Edition: 2016. Copyright © 2001 by Crossway, a publishing ministry of Good News Publishers. Used by permission. All rights reserved.

Scripture quotations marked NLT are taken from the *Holy Bible*, New Living Translation, copyright © 1996, 2004, 2015 by Tyndale House Foundation. Used by permission of Tyndale House Publishers, Inc., Carol Stream, Illinois 60188. All rights reserved.

Scripture quotations marked NIV are taken from the Holy Bible, NEW INTERNATIONAL VERSION®, NIV® Copyright © 1973, 1978, 1984, 2011 by Biblica, Inc.® Used by permission. All rights reserved worldwide.

Cover Design: Matt Naylor, Matt Naylor Graphic Design, mattnaylor.com
Interior Design and Typesetting: Gretchen Logterman

ISBN: 978-1-64507-163-1 (Print)
ISPN: 978-1-64507-164-8 (eBook)

Library of Congress Cataloging-in-Publication Data
Names: Thomas, Scott, 1959 November 22- author.
Title: The gospel shaped leader : leaning on Jesus to shepherd his people / Scott Thomas.
Description: Greensboro, NC : New Growth Press, [2021] | Includes bibliographical references. | Summary: "Scott Thomas, former director of Acts 29, church planter, and pastor unpacks how leaning on Jesus empowers not just your teaching, but also grows the humility, kindness, and biblical wisdom you need to lead"-- Provided by publisher.
Identifiers: LCCN 2021012746 | ISBN 9781645071631 (print) | ISBN 9781645071648 (ebook)
Subjects: LCSH: Christian leadership.
Classification: LCC BV652.1 .T4765 2021 | DDC 253--dc23
LC record available at https://lccn.loc.gov/2021012746

Printed in the United States of America
28 27 26 25 24 23 22 21   1 2 3 4 5

Contents

Foreword

O ne of my favorite lines, in one of my favorite movies, comes from *Rocky*. Rocky is about to go into the fight of his life with the world heavyweight champion. There is no point in bravado or swagger, and Rocky knows it. So, he says to Adrian, "I just want to go the distance." Whether he wins or loses, Rocky longs to fight well all the way. That's exactly how I feel, and I'm guessing you do too. Wherever you're serving the Lord, however you're advancing the gospel, you want to go the distance, you want your life to count, you want to bear "fruit that will last" (John 15:16 NIV).

How could you not feel that way? God created you, Christ died for you, and the Holy Spirit indwells you, for a *magnificent* purpose—that your life will display his glory now and forever. He sure isn't asking you to settle for mediocrity.

But let's *all* admit it. Sometimes we who sincerely want to serve the Lord can diminish our influence through patterns of leadership that just don't look like his glorious gentleness and wisdom and love—for starters.

Here's one way I try to stay focused on what's at stake in my high calling. These days I am blitzing through the Bible on a six-month reading plan. As I plow along day by day, I keep my place with a 3-by-5 card. On one side of the card I have written these two verses: "Now in a great house there are not only vessels of gold and silver but also of wood and clay, some for honorable use, some for dishonorable. Therefore, if anyone cleanses himself from what is dishonorable, he will be a vessel for honorable use, set apart as holy, useful to the master of the house, ready for every good work" (2 Timothy 2:20–21).

I love those verses. They remind me to stay open to the Lord, so that I can grow as a "vessel for honorable use" in his gracious hands.

My friend, whoever you are, by God's grace, you *can* go the distance—all the way. You *can* serve the Lord honorably. You *can* bear fruit that will last, both in this life and throughout the next—forever.

That is why my friend Scott Thomas wrote this book: to help you get there, and stay there, and enjoy the journey. *The Gospel Shaped Leader: Leaning on Jesus to Shepherd His People* comes from Scott's many years of experience in pastoring and leading. He knows what he's talking about. And he's good at it. The proof of his ministry is wonderfully obvious to all of us at Immanuel Church in Nashville.

I commend to you Scott's insightful book, not merely for your survival in ministry but for your joyous flourishing in ministry, and for the joy of the people you lead. If you'll keep leaning on Jesus to shepherd his people, how can that not go really, really well for you and everyone?

God be with you!

Ray Ortlund
Pastor to Pastors, Immanuel Church
President, Renewal Ministries

1.
WATCH

Gospel-Shaped Leaders Pay Careful Attention to Their Souls

> Much Christian leadership is exercised by people who do
> not know how to develop healthy, intimate relationships
> and have opted for power and control instead. Many
> Christian empire-builders have been people unable to give
> and receive love.
>
> Henri Nouwen, *In the Name of Jesus*

It's time to change how we lead our churches and Christian ministries. The current leadership model is not working. I'm not suggesting a new model, I'm calling for a return to the original plan demonstrated by Christ and commanded in Scripture. I'm writing to pastors, elders, deacons, church staff, small group leaders, and leaders of Christian ministries. Let's lead the Lord's church in the Lord's way. In short, we need gospel-shaped leaders leaning on Jesus to shepherd his people.

I watched an intelligent church leader self-destruct over enviousness, boastfulness, arrogance, and manipulative bullying. He had extraordinary success in ministry, but his spiritual immaturity capsized it. After years of browbeating his staff, church officers, and members, the church board finally enacted disciplinary action against him. The church removed him and it left a mess. I wish this were an isolated case. A church leader doesn't typically lose their role in a church for failing to fill the pews but, rather, for failing to get along with people. Gospel-shaped leadership is about guiding and managing others by using intertwined spiritual, emotional, and relational wisdom. Unfortunately, this isn't always taught in seminary, even though it is taught throughout Scripture.

Church leadership begins with how well leaders manage themselves according to the gospel. The gospel is good news that a holy God yearned with love for people guilty of disobedience against him. The compassionate Father sent his Son to live a sinless life and die to take our punishment. God raised him from the dead to secure the forgiveness of sins. Salvation and eternal life are for all who, by faith, repent and believe in Jesus as Lord and Savior. Through the return of Jesus, God will restore the creation to enjoy our new life with him forever.

As leaders shaped by the gospel, we are continually transformed from the inside out. We don't just proclaim the good news, we embody it through our life and how we lead others. In Jesus's economy, every Christian leader must demonstrate a changed life. William Tyndale describes the gospel as good, merry, glad, and joyful tidings that make our hearts glad and make us sing, dance, and leap for joy.[1] That's the good news we need in our churches. It emanates from the Spirit of God through his leaders.

Gospel-shaped leaders, therefore, would benefit from a daily examination of the condition of their soul. Our spiritual health affects us and everyone around us. Paul urged his protégé, Timothy, "Keep a close watch on yourself and on the teaching. Persist in this, for by so doing you will save both yourself and your hearers" (1 Timothy 4:16). Notice the words "close watch," "persist," and "save." These are not casual suggestions. These are wartime commands. Jesus said, "*Watch yourselves* lest your hearts be weighed down with dissipation and drunkenness and cares of this life, and that day come upon you suddenly like a trap. . . . *Stay awake* at all times, praying that you may have strength to escape all these things that are going to take place, and to stand before the Son of Man" (Luke 21:34, 36, emphasis added). Leaders must stay alert and be aware of their lives and those they lead.

Every church leader must engage in this spiritual battle with sober-mindedness, knowing the enemy seeks to destroy both shepherds and sheep. The prophet Zechariah warned, "Strike the shepherd, and the sheep will be scattered; I will turn my hand against the little ones" (Zechariah 13:7 [cf. Matthew 26:31]). Church leadership is not a position, nor is it a picnic. It is a spiritual war zone, and gospel-shaped leaders must come prepared with Christ's mind (Philippians 2:1–5) and the power of the Spirit (Romans 8:3–11).

When I first became a lead pastor thirty years ago, I pushed myself and others to achieve *my* goals for the church. I led the church with the business and marketing principles I knew. I emphasized numerical growth at the expense of spiritual growth. It wasn't until I discovered a consistent thread in the Bible of gospel-shaped leadership that I had a new perspective on how to lead. I regret not finding it earlier.

Formed by Something

Something is always forming our leadership. It may be success, control, approval, comfort, security, or something else. I worshiped success and it was forming me. Everybody worships something or someone and what we worship is what forms us. Acts 20 was instrumental for me to get gospel perspective. Paul's appeal to the Ephesian elders was twofold: pay careful attention to your lives as leaders and pay careful attention to those you lead (Acts 20:28). Simply stated, if as leaders we're unable to properly direct our own lives, we can't lead others. We best serve ourselves and others when we remove the mask and reveal our true selves to a gospel-reflecting mirror to measure our spiritual, emotional, relational, and vocational life. No leader has perfect health. I wasn't properly directing my own life, and I needed the gospel to reshape me.

Church leaders often cite ministry demands as a significant contributor to a lack of health in their family, finances, relationships, emotions, and bodies. But that's only an excuse to disregard self-leadership. We must see the extent of our leadership. If we merely pay careful attention to the flock (Acts 20:28), we're only doing half our job. What is missing, however, is life-threatening. Church leaders that make a wreck of their lives will inevitably make a wreck of the flock. Church leaders must pay careful attention to themselves while paying careful attention to those in their care.

This book is far from five steps to become a famous leader; it is about becoming a leader who reflects the gospel. Frankly, I prefer the term serving over leading to describe our role. Jesus said, "The greatest among you shall be your servant" (Matthew 23:11). I believe the posture of a leader reflects Christ's servanthood. If we apply these principles, it can help to bring meaning and beauty to our lives as we lead others. Every leader or aspiring leader can become more fruitful with focused intentionality on these principles. As it's been said, "This ain't rocket surgery." These principles are so simple that anyone can abide. That is the point. Leaders need to govern their lives based on reproducible and repeatable life principles. If we focus on productivity, we may compromise our principles. But if we focus on allowing the gospel to form our lives, we are more likely to be productive. It might even redefine how we measure productivity. Hopefully, it generates some rethinking of our practices and priorities because it is time to change the way we lead the church.

Healthy Soul

Only gospel-shaped Christian leaders can produce God-glorifying ministries. Formal education is critical to Christian leadership. However, I am convinced that traditional theological education *alone* is not enough for long-term, sustainable ministry. Christian leadership requires both spiritual maturity and emotional maturity to care for the church of God. An emotionally unsound leader or board member can derail an entire organization. I have seen it happen more than once. One pastor told me he had recently left his church because of illness. "Oh," I said compassionately, "what was the illness?" He responded, "The congregation got sick of me." This downfall wasn't his failure to apply the gospel to his preaching, but his failure to apply the gospel to his leadership and relationships. This, I have observed, is the missing factor for many church leaders.

Leaders always set the tone of an organization. An emotionally or spiritually weak leader will influence everyone else around them. We train everyone in our organization to be just like us (Luke 6:40). Caring for God's church (Acts 20:28) demands that we pay careful attention to ourselves and the people who the Holy Spirit entrusts to us.

I obtained a smart bathroom scale that revealed how naïve I was about my health. A non-smart scale measures your weight. That's it. A smart scale, on the other hand, provides data that can help you to get healthy. It enabled me to closely monitor my weight, body-fat percentage, muscle, protein, water, and stuff I didn't understand—like visceral fat, whatever that is. More than that, it helped me to lose body fat and gain muscle. This insider information led to action, which produced a more physically healthy person.

This book introduces twelve principles that can serve as a healthy gospel leadership smart scale. It is not enough to merely *know* the gospel. We must passionately, actively, and intentionally *live* the gospel in all facets of life, including our leadership. Paul prays that his reader would be "filled with the knowledge of [God's] will in all spiritual wisdom and understanding, so as to walk in a manner worthy of the Lord, fully pleasing to him: bearing fruit in every good work and increasing in the knowledge of God" (Colossians 1:9b–10). We have to measure our behavior, attitudes, and emotions in the less visible areas of our lives. This book will help us develop an action plan based on our self-examination. It might also provoke more profound contemplation through honest discussion with other believers. Staying honest with others will prompt us to become gospel-shaped leaders. And this desire to become a better leader leads to actions that open the door for change and gospel-shaped leadership.

Watch over the Church of God

Paul tells the elders at Ephesus, "Pay careful attention to yourselves and to all the flock, in which the Holy Spirit has made you overseers, to care for the church of God, which he obtained with his own blood" (Acts 20:28). The main idea in this passage is not to pay careful attention to yourselves or to pay careful attention to all of the flock. It is not even to defend against attacking wolves (Acts 20:29). The main idea in this passage is to care for the church of God—the church belonging to God that he obtained through the blood of Jesus. Care is the verb form of the Greek word translated shepherd or pastor. The leading biblical metaphor for church leadership is shepherding, although it's not always popular among Western churches. Have you ever seen a sheep in a pasture, after all? When church leaders embody a caring shepherding posture, they glorify the Chief Shepherd, Jesus, in their leadership. The apostle Peter adds to Paul's metaphor of a shepherding approach:

> So I exhort the elders among you, as a fellow elder and a witness of the sufferings of Christ, as well as a partaker in the glory that is going to be revealed: *shepherd the flock of God* that is among you, exercising oversight, not under compulsion, but willingly, as God would have you; not for shameful gain, but eagerly; not domineering over those in your charge, but *being examples to the flock*. And when the *chief Shepherd* appears, you will receive the unfading crown of glory. (1 Peter 5:1–4, emphasis added)

Paul and Barnabas appoint elders at every church during their travels through Derbe, Lystra, Iconium, and Antioch (Acts 14:23). The Holy Spirit appoints overseers (*episkopos*) through the affirmation of the local church (Acts 13) to shepherd the souls of those in their oversight (Acts 20:28). Overseer is a literal translation of the word *episkopos* (*epi* = over; *skopos* = seer). Paul elsewhere uses the word as a designation for elders or pastors (1 Timothy 3:1), so it seems to have become a technical term that is not inclusive of all church leaders. God's people are his beloved sheep, entrusted to the care of God's shepherds. Leaders must feel the sacredness of that charge before they can obey this calling to lead. The precious souls of our churches belong to God, obtained by the blood of Christ. Church leaders work under the authority and accountability of the Good Shepherd, Jesus (John 10:11, 14).

The North American church often celebrates the success of a church leader over their character, and their influence over their integrity. The Bible does the opposite. When our talent outweighs our character, it will eventually crush us. Spurgeon advised his students, "Our character must be more persuasive than our speech." He further accentuated, "It is not great talent God blesses so much as likeness to Jesus."[2] Danger is always nearby when we celebrate greatness over godliness. Godly character will produce fruitfulness in ministry.

Church leaders must take caution not to spend excessive time and energy attending to the flock's needs at the expense of their souls. Ministries are prone to celebrate performance-based metrics. Only spiritually vibrant leaders can lead the church God's way. A leader's ministry is to demonstrate how to be passionately dedicated to the Lord without self-centered obsession. In this way, the gospel shapes the leader.

Paul doesn't just say pay attention, but rather pay *careful* attention. The term is used elsewhere by Luke in the New Testament and translated "watch yourselves" (Luke 21:34–36), "beware" (Luke 12:1), and "pay attention to yourselves"

(Luke 17:1–3). Jesus uses the term to warn believers to "*beware* of false prophets, who come to you in sheep's clothing" (Matthew 7:15). And he cautions that he will send them out as "sheep in the midst of wolves. . . . *Beware* of men, for they will deliver you over to courts and flog you in their synagogues" (Matthew 10:16–17). Followers do not naturally take careful thought of others around them; leaders do. Consider how you would pay close attention to the activities of a two-year-old child near a busy street. You would not take your eyes off the toddler. In a similar way, we must pay careful attention to ourselves and to those we lead.

Paul urges the elders at Ephesus to pay careful attention to *ourselves* while we pay careful attention *to the flock of God* the Holy Spirit entrusts to our care. We cannot neglect others, and we cannot neglect ourselves if we want to properly care for those in the church.

Significance of Emotional Health and Leadership Effectiveness

One way those outside the church try to explain leadership maturity is through what psychologists describe as emotional intelligence (or EQ), which is fundamentally biblical wisdom and gospel formation. Emotional intelligence is the ability to identify, comprehend, and manage the emotions in self and others. This ability guides one's attitude and actions. Ministry is all about managing self and relating to others. Emotional intelligence is not taught in the church or seminary but is central to church leadership effectiveness. The leadership principles that follow rest on the gospel's foundation and view it through the secondary lens of wisdom about our emotions. I believe the gospel is necessary to understand our emotions.

Dr. Daniel Goleman is a psychologist and author of the *New York Times* bestsellers *Emotional Intelligence: Why It Can Matter More Than IQ* and *Social Intelligence: The New Science of Human Relationships*. Goleman posits that emotional intelligence is the prerequisite of leadership. He writes, "Without it, a person can have the best training in the world, an incisive, analytical mind, and an endless supply of smart ideas, but he [or she] still won't make a great leader."[3] Church leadership requires gospel-shaped values like gentleness, humility, and ongoing repentance.

In an interview, some church leaders asked my wife how she was handling her chronic kidney disease. She tearfully shared her traumatic and prolonged journey. One leader interrupted her and proceeded to tell about a medical condition that he had experienced many years earlier. The group stared at him in shocked disbelief as he unwittingly hijacked the conversation and redirected it away from her and toward himself. He never acknowledged her emotional pain and openness in sharing it. He appears to be competent; yet it's unlikely he will be useful to the degree he could unless he learns to exercise gospel compassion.

Leaders unable to empathetically join in another person's story—good or bad—will not influence at the deepest level.

Improving Emotional and Spiritual Health

Emotional intelligence is the willingness to process our emotions and experiences. Church leaders often lack an outlet to share their painful experiences. It is healthy to navigate our spiritual and emotional journey with others. Church leaders need a safe place to share their struggles. It is my prayer that this book will open that door between friends. Church leaders need a coach, mentor, or friend with whom they can share their challenges.

Sometimes highly intelligent leaders are perplexed as to why they do not experience the level of success they would like to see. They seem to lack the "right stuff" necessary for the outcomes they desire. It is not technical skills, like parsing Greek verbs, they lack, but more like the ability to express love, joy, and grace. Goleman believes that effective leaders *all* have emotional intelligence.[4]

Goleman went through several iterations to explain emotional intelligence, eventually refining the model into four domains: (1) self-awareness, (2) self-management, (3) social awareness, (4) relationship management. We will explore these concepts throughout the book as they apply to the context of leading with the gospel.

Four Emotional Intelligence Domains

Emotional intelligence is not the foundation of healthy, biblical leadership; the gospel is the foundation. But we will use an EQ metric to see the gospel with clarity and identify areas where we might not be walking in step with the gospel (Galatians 2:14). In the following table, the first two domains (left column) fall under the category of paying careful attention to ourselves (Acts 20:28). These competencies are tools to measure how well we pay careful attention to our souls. The second couplet of domains (right column) addresses paying careful attention to the flock. These competencies are tools to measure how well we pay careful attention to the flock that God has entrusted to us.

Pay Careful Attention to Yourself	Pay Careful Attention to All the Flock
Self-Awareness	Relational Awareness
"For by the grace given to me I say to everyone among you not to think of himself more highly than he ought to think, but to think with sober judgment, each according to the measure of faith that God has assigned" (Rom. 12:3).	"For the whole law is fulfilled in one word: 'You shall love your neighbor as yourself'" (Gal. 5:14).
I am growing in my understanding of my emotions and moods (1 Cor. 13:12) and allowing God to test and refine them (Ps. 26:2). I am learning how they affect others around me (Lam. 3:40). I know my limitations and can assess my strengths by faith (Rom. 12:3; 1 John 1:8). I am confident in the Lord's redeeming work in me and am patient in my progress (2 Tim. 1:6–7).	I am thoughtful of others around me and am compassionate about their needs (Matt. 9:35–38). I listen to others as an act of love and can discern their unspoken actions, attitudes, and emotions (1 John 4:1; Phil. 1:9–10). I seek to communicate with straightforwardness, transparency, and honesty (Matt. 5:37).
1. DIE: Sacrifice to Make a Difference	7. LOVE: Love the Church
2. WALK: Embrace Their Father's Love	8. SERVE: Lead with Humility
3. PLAN: Design Their Life with God's Purpose	9. SPEAK: Communicate with Grace-Filled Candor

Self-Management	Relational Management
"[You were taught] to put off your old self, which belongs to your former manner of life and is corrupt through deceitful desires, and to be renewed in the spirit of your minds, and to put on the new self, created after the likeness of God in true righteousness and holiness" (Eph. 4:22–24).	"I therefore, a prisoner for the Lord, urge you to walk in a manner worthy of the calling to which you have been called, with all humility and gentleness, with patience, bearing with one another in love, eager to maintain the unity of the Spirit in the bond of peace" (Eph. 4:1–3).
I am submitting my mind, will, and emotions to the desires of the Spirit and not to the desires of the flesh (Gal. 5:16–26). The gospel is continually shaping me (Phil. 1:27) through the power of the Spirit (Rom. 8:4–11), and I am confessing my sins and acknowledging my weaknesses (1 John 1:7–9). I am striving for holiness and the renewing of my mind that leads to a transformed life (Rom. 12:1–2). With my hope in Jesus, I'm patient in my hardships and constant in my prayer (Rom. 12:12).	I can apply biblical wisdom in relational circumstances (James 1:5). I commit to develop other people to build up the organization (Eph. 4:11, 16). I seek to resolve relational conflicts (Phil. 4:2). I seek to reconcile my broken relationships (Matt. 5:23–24; 18:15; Rom. 12:18). I can build relationships to accomplish goals (Heb. 10:24–25).
4. STAND: Pursue Integrity Always	10. GUIDE: Relate as Family
5. LEARN: Explore New Ideas	11. COACH: Develop Other Leaders
6. REST: Commit to a Sabbath	12. YOKE: Grow Meaningful Friendships

Google's Shocking Revelation

Google revealed a shocking fact about its employees when it tested its hiring hypothesis dating back to the company's incorporation in 1998. It analyzed every bit and byte of hiring, firing, and promotion data through Project Oxygen. The results were shocking. Expertise in science, technology, engineering, and mathematics (STEM) came in dead last in a list of the most important qualities of Google's top employees. The six characteristics of success at Google, according to this research, are all soft skills:

1. Coaching
2. Communicating and listening well
3. Possessing insights into others (including others' different values and points of view)
4. Having empathy toward and being supportive of one's colleagues
5. Being an excellent critical thinker and problem solver
6. Being able to make connections across complex ideas.[5]

Google may have identified the value of soft skills. However, Scripture already codified the importance of these gospel expressions. For instance, I grew up in a home where I was encouraged to be aggressive and successful. I brought those values into church ministry and quickly realized they didn't work. However, when I studied the ministry of Jesus, I noticed that he asked questions and approached people with gentleness. When I became aware of my emotions and how they affected others, it was a game-changer ministry-wise.

The apostle Paul disparages those who may possess abilities and skills but are devoid of love (1 Corinthians 13). Paul describes love in ways that resonate with sixteen characteristics typically associated with Bible-based soft skills. He describes love as:

1. Patient
2. Kind

3. Compassionate (not envious)
4. Modest (not boastful)
5. Humble (not arrogant)
6. Gentle (not rude)
7. Tolerant (not demanding)
8. Good-humored (not irritable)
9. Pleasant
10. Forgiving
11. Virtuous
12. Truthful
13. Protecting
14. Trusting
15. Hopeful
16. Persevering

These foundational characteristics describing love will benefit leaders. A gospel-shaped leader will radiate the essential characteristics of love. Love is the one verifiable characteristic that demonstrates our connection to Christ, the one who loves us (John 13:34–35). Ray Ortlund Jr. recalled that his father used to say that a person comes into a room with the attitude of "Here I am" or "There you are." The difference is stark. The two postures demonstrate where our love resides: in ourselves or in Christ toward others.

Another example of Bible-based emotional intelligence is found in the Beatitudes. Jesus promises a flourishing life to those who are poor in spirit, mourners, meek, merciful, pure in heart, peacemakers, and able to rest in God amid challenges (Matthew 5:2–12).

Become a Gospel-Shaped Leader

What is foremost in Paul's mind in Acts 20 seems to be guarding against false teaching. Paul's concern is with "men speaking twisted things, to draw away the disciples after them" (Acts 20:30). Paul encourages Timothy, "Keep a close watch on yourself and on the teaching. Persist in this, for by so doing, you will save both yourself and your hearers" (1 Timothy 4:16).

Others are counting on us. Paying careful attention and keeping a close watch is hard work, but we and others will benefit immensely. We can't do this alone. Other than family, I believe we as leaders need four people in our lives:

1. A friend to have fun together. "A joyful heart is good medicine, but a crushed spirit dries up the bones" (Proverbs 17:22). Don't miss this vital relationship.
2. An advocate to look out for our best interests and one who will open their mouth when we need something (Proverbs 31:8–9).
3. A coach to help guide our life and ministry (Hebrews 3:12–13; 10:24–25).
4. A confidant with whom we can be completely honest without consequence (1 John 1:7).

The church leader mentioned at the beginning of the chapter had none of these people in his life. He pushed friends away, he advocated for himself, and misused church funds. No coach was good enough or smart enough in his perspective, and the only confidants he had were employed directly under him, which never works.

Christ shapes our hearts and character with the gospel. He uses others to help watch the condition of our souls. But we have to be daring enough to take off our masks and let others see our true condition.

Your Turn . . .

Prayer for a Healthy Soul

Lord, I have weaknesses that invade my heart and mind on a regular basis. They invade me with such fervor that I tremble at their persistence. You are Lord over every one of your church leaders. You created me to care for your flock and want me to care for my soul. Empower me to shepherd the flock of God that is among me and to be an example to the flock. You are the Shepherd and Overseer of my soul. When I stray, draw me back into your fold.

Coaching Questions

You will benefit from reflecting on what you read. We don't usually do this because our goal is often to finish what we're reading. This book aims to prompt you to think differently about an idea or concept and then take specific action steps. Inspiration gives birth to contemplation. Contemplation leads to action. Action opens the door for change. And change leads to influence.

Several questions are included at the end of each chapter. These questions work best when you interact with other people around the subjects. By doing this, you will analyze the leadership practices in your life even as you deepen friendships. This book could serve as a resource for a group of people to be "mutually encouraged by each other's faith" (Romans 1:12). It might also grow meaningful friendships (see chapter 13).

Questions:

1. What do you believe are the essential characteristics of a leader who embodies the gospel?
2. How does the concept of shepherd leadership change the way you would approach practical leadership?
3. Read the healthy leadership descriptions on the table in this chapter and rate your emotional intelligence in each of the four major domains from 1 (poor) to 5 (excellent). Explain your ratings.

Self-awareness	1	2	3	4	5
Self-management	1	2	3	4	5
Relational awareness	1	2	3	4	5
Relational management	1	2	3	4	5

4. Which of the twelve principles on the table do you need to focus on the most at this time? How is the gospel evident in these principles?
5. Why is a gospel-shaped leader crucial to the church?
6. What is your first step to becoming a healthier leader who pays careful attention to the condition of your soul? Be specific.

Part One

Self-Awareness

For by the grace given to me I say to everyone among you
not to think of himself more highly than he ought to think,
but to think with sober judgment, each according to the
measure of faith that God has assigned.

Romans 12:3

Self-Awareness. I am growing in my understanding of my emotions and moods (1 Corinthians 13:12) and am allowing God to test and refine them (Psalm 26:2). I am learning how they affect others around me (Lamentations 3:40). I know my limitations and can assess my strengths by faith (Romans 12:3; 1 John 1:8). I am confident in the Lord's redeeming work in me and am patient in my progress (2 Timothy 1:6–7).

2.
DIE

Gospel-Shaped Leaders Sacrifice to Make a Difference

I have one desire now—to live a life of reckless abandon for the Lord, putting all my energy and strength into it.

Elisabeth Elliot, *Through Gates of Splendor*

Gospel-shaped leaders are aware of their identity in Christ. They see themselves as servants who sacrifice for the good of others, just as Christ did. Self-aware leaders do not think of themselves more highly than they ought. Rather, they are aware of their assignment proceeding from God for the good of his people (Romans 12:3).

A young man, successful in business, became an elder of the church where I was lead pastor. He was a gifted communicator who led a large Sunday school class, but he began to use his influence to debase the other elders. He had looks, charm, and intelligence, but he lacked humility because he wasn't aware of his insatiable thirst for power. Each of the other six elders had been in the church for over twenty years. He didn't have the same respect of the congregation, but it was growing. He recruited two young elders and they began a slandering campaign aimed at the older elders. They told their circle of influence that the men were not qualified to be elders.

The younger men used Bible verses out of context and walked around with an air of spiritual superiority. Their coalition intimidated others. The older elders were not aware of their subtle gossip. The trio held secret meetings and documented their plan. I found their written documents in the church copier. I stood between them and the other elders. They were relentless and unified for over a year. It negatively affected my ability to lead, so I asked them privately to resign but they declined. In an elder's meeting, I brought up their need to resign and they again refused. The older elders didn't recognize the gravity of the situation, so I resigned. It was one of the biggest mistakes I made in ministry. In hindsight, I learned that by resigning I had sacrificed others for my good. I thought I was making a statement to the church by resigning. I was unaware of my immature approach and how it would discourage the church in their pursuit of the gospel. Jesus says, "Greater love has no one than this, that someone lay down his life for his friends" (John 15:13). If we sacrifice others for our good, we are wolves rather than shepherds (Acts 20:28-29). But when we surrender our lives for others' good, we put the gospel on display. At the end of the chapter, I will explore how I would address this differently today.

If we're not willing to sacrifice our lives for the good of God's people, we're not ready for leadership in the church. Leadership is not self-serving; it is others-serving. Jesus says, "The Son of Man came not to be served but to serve, and to give his life as a ransom for many" (Matthew 20:28). Jesus warns his disciples not to live for selfish pursuits because it would result in insignificance and loss (Matthew 16:25; cf., Mark 8:35; Luke 9:24). Jesus offers a refreshing alternative. If we choose a sacrificial life—after the gospel's pattern—our lives will make a difference. Jesus tells his disciples he *must* suffer many things, be rejected, and killed. If we're not willing to face suffering, rejection, and death to self, we're not willing to follow Jesus.

When God's Spirit indwells leaders, they envision and dream of a better future for others. Children imagine being firefighters, police, princesses, and Olympic athletes. They see themselves as valued instruments to make life better for others. Somewhere in our image-bearing self, we have an innate desire to make our lives count for something. We desire to influence, create, conquer, achieve, build, protect, and rescue. Most people want to help others. We imagine walking through fire-engulfed buildings rescuing children or animals. We discover or create something for the good of others. We imagine carrying people on our backs to do what they may never have achieved without our sacrifice. In short, we envision our life making a difference for others.

We may have forgotten about serving others in our pursuit to serve ourself. How can we regain that desire to sacrifice our lives for the good of others? What would it take to trade our life's goals, ambitions, savings, and talents to advance the gospel in others' lives? A gospel leader seeks to promote others at the expense of self. We either empty ourselves daily, or we will become full of ourselves.

Leaders experience frustration at times. One might say, "This is not what God designed me to do with my life, but I can't figure out a way to make a change." If a leader is emotionally frustrated, chances are the people around that leader are feeling it as well. Assess why you are frustrated. It may be that you are being self-centered rather than serving God and others. C. S. Lewis said, "The terrible thing, the almost impossible thing, is to hand over your whole self—all your wishes and precautions—to Christ."[1] Be willing to die to your natural pleasure so others may live. This may not be the dramatic rescuing of a child from a burning building. It is more likely to mean postponing an anniversary date to reach out to a husband/father who just left his family. Or it might mean going to the ER on a Saturday night to be with an elderly church member who has been in a car crash. It could also mean sacrificing a dream vacation to invest in a mission.

Sacrifice for a Cause

Jesus says, "This is my commandment, that you love one another as I have loved you. Greater love has no one than this, that someone lay down his life for his friends" (John 15:12–13). Jesus is not primarily speaking of our sacrificial love for others, though that is secondary. He speaks of how he would demonstrate his love for us by laying down his life for us. His life, death, and resurrection are payment in full on our behalf to satisfy a holy God and free us from the consequences of guilt (Romans 3:24; Galatians 4:4–5; Colossians 1:14). God in human flesh died so he could save humankind from eternal death.

The late 13th-century English army oppressed the residents of Scotland, regularly overpowering their diminutive army. In the movie *Braveheart*, William Wallace, played by Mel Gibson, is a leader in the Wars of Scottish Independence. Before leading the skittish Scots into battle, he says: "I see a whole army of my countrymen, here in defiance of tyranny. You've come to fight as free men and free men you are. What will you do without freedom? Will you fight?" One man responds while pointing at the vast English army, "Against that? No, we will run, and we will live." Wallace gives a spirited retort, "Fight and you may die. Run, and you'll live—at least for a while. And dying in your beds many years from now, would you be willing to trade all the days, from this day to that, for one chance—just one chance—to come back here and tell our enemies that they may take our lives, but they will never take our freedom."[2]

In the movie, Wallace chooses to lose his life for the chance to gain freedom for his countrymen. He inspires them to fight against impossible odds. The alternative is to continue to live without hope under the oppression and abuse of the English regime. Wallace loses his own life, but the movie portrays him as making a significant difference—a difference for the good of many others. The Bible talks about someone else who sacrificed for the good of others.

Behold the Lamb of God

At the beginning of his earthly ministry, Jesus arrives at the Jordan River, where John the Baptist is baptizing new believers. John curtails his sermonic discourse when he sees Jesus walking toward him. John exclaims, "Behold, the Lamb of God, who takes away the sin of the world!" (John 1:29b). John is referring to the Old Testament sacrificial system of atonement for sins. Atonement means making amends, blotting out the offense, and giving satisfaction for the wrong done. Atonement reconciles the hopelessly guilty person with the holy Creator who hates sin and must punish it (Jeremiah 44:4; Romans 2:5–9). When God brings Israel out of Egypt, he sets up a system of sacrifices as part of the covenant relationship.

God's people offer unflawed animals in exchange for atonement, the removal of their sins (Leviticus 17:11). The sacrifices are repeated year after year. They are a shadow and type of the promised Lamb who would take away sins once and for all (Hebrews 10:11; Romans 3:25–26). John the Baptist knew that Lamb, the antitype, the sinless Son of God had arrived, but this time it was different: "But when Christ had offered for all time a single sacrifice for sins, he sat down at the right hand of God, waiting from that time until his enemies should be made a footstool for his feet. For by a single offering he has perfected for all time those who are being sanctified" (Hebrews 10:12–14).

On the cross, in obedience to his Father, Jesus cries out, "It is finished" (John 19:30), and he bows his head and dies. The cry is translated by the single Greek word *tetelstai* (τετέλεσται) meaning "paid in full." It means to bring to an end, complete, accomplish, fulfill, pay, finish. Jesus became the payment in full. He died as our sacrificial Lamb. His action provided a right relationship between God and humankind. His death once and for all time paid sin's penalty in full. It did not demand repeat sacrifices. The real sacrifice, the perfect Lamb of God, from that point on, was visible and available to all.

Necessity of Sacrifice

Jesus says, "Greater love has no one than this, that someone lay down his life for his friends" (John 15:13). In almost every culture since the beginning of time, sacrificing one's life in order that others may live has been regarded as the ultimate act of courage and selflessness. Understandably, it's an act few people are ever willing to make. Most every significant event includes sacrifice at some level. Life comes after sacrifice. Resurrection occurs after death.

In 2018 in France, a radical terrorist attacked a grocery store. The terrorist had already killed two people and was holding other hostages. Lieutenant Colonel Arnaud Beltrame, of the French military police, walked in unarmed and offered the terrorist his life in exchange for the release of one female hostage. The hostage was safely released, but Lieutenant Colonel Arnaud Beltrame was shot to death by the terrorist who claimed allegiance to a religious ideology. A Canadian newspaper reported the story with the headline, "Once again, a man dies so that others may be saved." The article remarked, "When [the female hostage's] Friday morning began, she did not think that she would need a savior that day. She was going to buy groceries. But she found herself held hostage by a murderous terrorist. And she needed to be saved."[3] This secular newspaper made a strong connection between the sacrificial acts of a human and a divine Savior. Our acts of sacrifice are more evident to the skeptical watching world than we realize. The newspaper added, "Arnaud's widow insists his sacrifice cannot be understood apart from his Christian faith." His life was in Christ and so was his death.

What causes are you willing to die for? Answering this could be a life-changing question. As a young man, I naïvely equated leadership with being in charge. This was the position held by the owner, the boss, the one who played golf in the middle of the workday. This may be the world's spin on leadership, but it is not biblical. The world believes leaders ascend, whereas Jesus teaches that leaders descend. Jesus walks in on a discussion the disciples are having among themselves about who would be the greatest. He redefines true leadership for them by saying: "The kings of the Gentiles exercise lordship over them, and those in authority over them are called bene-factors. But not so with you. Rather, let the greatest among you become as the youngest, and the leader as one who serves" (Luke 22:25–26).

What are you doing, or preparing to do, to benefit others? If nothing comes to mind, you may be busy dying one day at a time. You are not alone, and you are not stuck in this rut forever if you choose a life of self-sacrifice. It is never too late to begin. Some people choose good over great, leisure over life, fear over fight, and mundane over meaningful. For instance, we might not start that second service or invest in a church plant. We might resist sending fifty people to start a new ministry. We spend more time looking at the bottom line than at eternal life. Respond to opportunities that make a difference. Those opportunities usually require personal sac-rifice. Sacrifice does not mean death; it means dying to self and living to Christ. With Christ's life within us, we are free to sacrifice ourselves without fear.

Sacrifice Demands Risk-Taking Action

How is God leading you to sacrifice for others? What would get you out of bed with enthusiasm each day? Can you envi-sion what this would be? If so, have you put it into writing? Have you created a battle plan to complete it? Passion is fer-tilizer for risk-taking action. But passion without a plan is just cow manure. No person goes into battle without first devising a plan (Luke 14:31). Your life's purpose does not always have to equate to your vocation. Your vocation may be the means to allow you the time or the funds for your calling. Your sacrificial response to a call of God is your difference-making factor. What will you do with your ideas? Most people throw them out with the trash and make excuses. "They are not realistic," we may repeatedly say to ourselves.

"Be missed if you're gone," said bestselling author and business consultant Seth Godin.[4] He implored that right now may be the time for us to attempt something that we have always considered. Now is the time to stop being passive. It's natural to have fears. But we must act where we can make a difference. No more excuses. Sacrifice for the good of others. Be willing to die to self so others can live.

Chris and Yanci McGregor met at Dallas Seminary. After getting their master's degrees and marrying, they joined the staff at Fellowship Church in Dallas, one of America's largest churches. After ten years as pastor and worship leader, respectively, Chris and Yanci believed God was calling them to start a new church in Montreal, Canada, Chris's home country. In Montreal, less than one percent of the population attends an evangelical church. It was a daring sacrifice to leave jobs they loved and respond to this calling. City Church in Montreal now has two services to accommodate the number of people the Lord has brought to their care.

I opened the chapter by talking about my ministry mistake concerning an elder. Applying the principles described in this chapter, I should have been willing to stand between the wolf-like elders and the congregation. Instead, I fled and left the sheep to be ravaged by the enemy, in direct violation of John 10:12–15. If I had it to do over, I would have not only confronted the slanderous elders, but I would have included the other elders to appeal, pray, weep, and plead with them. If the sinning elders refused to repent, I would have fought to have them publicly removed from the sacred and holy office of elder. Not wanting to cause division in the church, I hesitated to take it this far and decided to leave the church. After that, the church split anyway. I am now more self-aware of how the gospel informs a sacrificial response for God's glory.

When Jesus sacrificed his life for us, he made an eternal difference. When we sacrifice for others, we make a difference.

Your Turn . . .

Prayer for Making a Difference

Lord, you gave your life to release me from the penalty of my sin. Your death set me free from condemnation. You became the Lamb that took away my sins once and for all. I can't contribute to the payment. It satisfied a Holy God. It is finished on the cross. Allow me the honor to serve others sacrificially. I give you my all, holding nothing back. I am yours to use as a living sacrifice—to be and do what you desire. Help me to make a difference for your glory.

Coaching Questions

1. As a child, what dreams did you have for your future?
2. How do those dreams relate to what you are doing now?
3. What ideas have you set aside that you would like to explore or attempt?
4. Where can you sacrifice to give yourself entirely to God and for the service of others?

3.
WALK

Gospel-Shaped Leaders Embrace Their Father's Love

> In our troubles, anxieties, perplexities, the longer I live the
> more am I impressed with the wisdom of speaking more to
> God and less to man. He can do more in the way of helping
> through all our difficulties than all others put together.
> Talk more with God, less with man.
>
> Francis Grimké, *Meditations on Preaching*

I grew up in a performance-based community. I only received love when I excelled at something. My dad worked until he was ninety years old. When he was eighty-nine, I asked him why he didn't quit. He said, with a gruff voice, "If a man doesn't work, what's he good for?" It was at that moment that I realized why I was so hard on myself. I didn't think I was any good at being a Christian because of my frequent failings and, therefore, I wasn't deserving of God's love. As a young leader, I tried to *earn* love from God and others through my accomplishments. I led people to Jesus and only expected love if I exceeded their expectations. I also expected others to keep up with me and I only affirmed them when they did. This prevented me from having deep relationships with others.

When I discovered that the gospel was more than the four spiritual laws, it set me free to live and lead in grace. I no longer led *to be* accepted. I led *from* my acceptance by God. Because of Christ, I was no longer a slave working tirelessly; I was now a beloved son of a loving Father. He is not prodding me to do more. He is embracing me in my weaknesses and walking with me as I lead others toward him.

Spiritual intimacy with God is a common struggle for many Christian leaders, but it's vital if we're to effectively lead. We must lead out of our identities as God's beloved children. Our relationship to our Father shapes how we lead his children. We lead others as we are led by the Father.

Intimacy is an authentic openness to others about feelings, beliefs, actions, and needs. Intimacy is elusive for people who may have experienced little to no affection as a child or young adult. Leaders may aspire to success and positions of influence to fill this emotional or spiritual void, commonly resulting from a broken relationship with their parents. They may not have ever trusted others with their emotions, or they may have been ridiculed, shamed, belittled, or victimized by family members. God the Father understands and fills this void with his love as displayed in the gospel.

Self-awareness is a growing understanding of one's emotions and moods. It starts with an awareness of our identity with the Father. Are we a slave or a son? Effective leaders are aware of how their actions, behaviors, and attitudes affect others around them. When we're aware of our limitations, we can lead by faith in a God who uses less-than-perfect vessels. Look closely at Paul's words for the kinds of leaders God chooses:

> God chose what is *foolish* in the world to shame the
> wise; God chose what is *weak* in the world to shame

the strong; God chose what is *low* and *despised* in the world, even *things that are not*, to bring to nothing things that are, so that no human being might boast in the presence of God. And because of him you are in Christ Jesus, who became to us wisdom from God, righteousness and sanctification and redemption, so that, as it is written, "Let the one who boasts, boast in the Lord." (1 Corinthians 1:27–31, emphasis added)

I regularly walk with a friend who is on staff with me. In meetings during the day we have an agenda and deadlines to complete our projects. But when we walk, we engage in each other's lives. Nothing rushes us. We walk at a steady pace as we listen and love, converse and care, laugh and learn. Spiritual intimacy can't be rushed but must be prioritized. In our immaturity, we expect instant results. Why do we so often grow impatient in the school of faith?

Prodigal Son

Love, which we all need and want, is a basic and powerful human need. The Bible tells us that God is love. While we usually emphasize our love for others, we have to start with God's love for us: "We love because he first loved us" (1 John 4:19). Understanding God's love for us is foundational to our ability to love others and being able to receive love. We see this in the story of the prodigal son in Luke 15.

Jesus told a beautiful story of an unexpected embrace by the father of a rebellious son, but we may miss the real beauty of the story if we only focus on the son. Prodigal can indeed mean wasteful or careless. It can also refer to someone who is extravagant in giving, overflowing in graciousness, abundant in tenderness and love. So this story could also be the parable of the prodigal father—or more descriptively, the parable of the father's overflowing, relentless love.

A parable is a story that helps shed light on a divine principle. Luke 15 records three parables to address the one accusation the Pharisees make against Jesus: "This man receives [welcomes] sinners and eats with them" (Luke 15:2). Each of the three parables—a lost sheep, a lost coin, and a lost son—illustrates how God welcomes the lost and celebrates the found. In the parable about the two sons, the younger son asks his father for an uncustomary advance on his inheritance. This son no longer wants to walk with his father or be under his care, teaching, or employment.

To make matters worse, he wants to cripple his father's wealth and the ongoing family business by demanding his financial inheritance. The father obliges, even though he recognizes the son's self-centeredness. He has to know it would not end well, yet he allows his son to make his decision. The outcome of the son's choices is predictable.

The stubborn son goes into a foreign country and wastes all of his money on a partying lifestyle. He self-destructs. When the economy weakens, the son is destitute. His job is feeding pigs—an ironic job for a Jew who considered pigs to be unclean animals (Leviticus 11:7). He becomes so hungry that he craves the pig slop, and apparently, no one cares enough to alleviate his hardship.

Four things are interesting, thus far in Jesus's story. First, the prodigal son is in dire need. His money gone, he finds himself unable to meet his basic needs. Second, his attempts to provide for himself are not sufficient. When pig slop looks appetizing, one is truly hungry. Third, no one gives him anything. Others feel no compassion for his plight. He is hungry, he is alone, and nobody seems to care. Fourth, amid his hardship he comes to his senses. Personal calamity leads to the prodigal's repentance.

We all possess a low-grade stubbornness by nature, and we finally come to our senses when we are lonely, needy, rejected, or neglected. Repentance is a gift from God. Repentance occurs not only when Christ converts a sinner, but every day of a believer's life in Christ, for that is what the Lord's Prayer teaches us in the fifth petition: "forgive us our debts, as we also have forgiven our debtors" (Matthew 6:12). The Lord taught us to ask forgiveness for all past sins that the Holy Spirit brings to our remembrance, and even the multitude of sins that we fail to remember. John Calvin said, "Not only is it fitting to confess those sins which we commit daily, but graver offenses ought to draw us further and recall to our minds those which seem long since buried."[1]

On the one hand, when we are aware of our weaknesses and sins yet make excuses, we demonstrate our emotional immaturity. On the other hand, when we recognize our failures and go to the one who can forgive us, we act with gospel-informed emotional and spiritual maturity. God is our Father who longs to heal and forgive us. Humankind seeks justice while God desires mercy for his people. God says, "I will not execute my burning anger; I will not again destroy Ephraim [Israel]; for I am God and not a man, the Holy One in your midst, and I will not come in wrath" (Hosea 11:9). God is not the executioner by nature. He is the embracer.

Prodigal Father

The prodigal son knows he has sinned against his father. He plans to ask his father if he can become his employee. Perhaps he thinks that his father would have enough mercy to hire him. He firmly does not believe he deserves his father's love or has even a remote chance to be treated as a son. Jewish law permitted a father to have the elders of the city stone to death a rebellious or stubborn son (Deuteronomy 21:18–21). To be allowed to live and get a job, one that does not involve pigs, would be more than plenty for the prodigal. Isn't it interesting that our entitlement often diminishes in proportion to our level of brokenness?

The son has sinned. He has no advocate, no friend, no wealth, no merit, and no family. Jesus, illuminating the beauty of the gospel, says, "He arose and came to his father. But while he was still a long way off, his father saw him and felt compassion, and ran and embraced him and kissed him" (Luke 15:20). Remember, prodigal means recklessly extravagant. Prodigality is what the father demonstrates to his rebellious son. His reckless and extravagant embrace and the lingering kiss is mind-boggling. The lavish love of the prodigal's father is in stark contrast to the son's excessive rebellion.

The son has a script that he plans to recite (Luke 15:18–19). He starts into it, and it's as if his father places his hand against his mouth and says, "Hush, my son, it's all right now." He does not have a chance to fall at his father's feet, begging for mercy as he intends. Instead, the father embraces the repentant son and kisses him. The father's compassion—his love, forgiveness, restoration, and joy—for his son is more shocking than his son's transgression. I picture the father putting all of his weight on his son. Both of them fall to the ground in an emotional embrace. The father initiates this loving embrace toward his unworthy son. Imagine this exchange of affection for the sinful son. Now imagine our Lord receiving you in this way after rebelling against him (Psalm 51:4).

The son finally speaks and declares he was not worthy of being treated like a son. But the father refuses to acknowledge that. Instead, he asks for the most elegant robe of the house to be wrapped around him—a picture of Christ's righteousness covering our filthy, pigpen-reeking lives. The father puts a ring on the son's finger. This ring likely has the family signet crafted on it—a symbol of the son's identity as a family member, not as a slave. The father gives the son sandals so that he may walk with the father once again. And the father kills the fattened calf, which was generally reserved for atonement (reparation for wrong-doing)—a representation of what truly has happened. To summarize, the son rebels, walks away, becomes destitute, and returns to his father expecting to be received as a slave but is instead welcomed as a son. We get to lead people in a similar way.

The Father's Embrace

The father's embrace was a gift of grace. The embrace was a physical manifestation of the gospel, the good news for a lost son. Our heavenly Father's love guides us back when ministry gets discouraging. His embrace is our safe place when we fear, lack faith, or fail. The gospel doesn't give us what we deserve or what we want; it gives us *more* than we can ever imagine. William Cowper wrote some of the church's best hymns. He wrote "O for a Closer Walk with God" in 1772 to illustrate that we may have left the Father's embrace, but he never abandons us (Hebrews 13:5). The first, second, and fifth stanzas remind us of the purpose of our walk with God:

> O for a closer walk with God,
> a calm and heav'nly frame,
> a light to shine upon the road
> that leads me to the Lamb!
>
> Where is the blessedness I knew
> when first I sought the Lord?
> Where is the soul refreshing view
> of Jesus and His Word?
>
> . . . .
>
> The dearest idol I have known,
> whate'er that idol be,
> help me to tear it from Thy throne
> and worship only Thee.
> (William Cowper, "O for a Closer Walk with God")

This embrace of the Father is felt deep within our souls. It is a second chance, redemption, hope. God may have allowed us to experience loss, but we will never lose his love. The writer of Hebrews says,

> God is treating you as sons. For what son is there whom his father does not discipline? If you are left without discipline . . . then you are illegitimate children and not sons. . . . But he disciplines us for our good, that we may share his holiness. For the moment all discipline seems painful rather than pleasant, but later it yields the peaceable fruit of

righteousness to those who have been trained by it.
(Hebrews 12:7, 8, 10b, 11)

We have a Father who loves us, and he proves it with corrective and perfectly timed measures in our lives.

The Recklessly Extravagant (Prodigal) Leader

We do not deserve the warm, welcoming embrace of the Father amid our sin. That's the point of the gospel. But every day we're invited into the arms of a compassionate Father to walk with him as his child, even if we're occasionally (or repeatedly) stubborn, rebellious, or defiant. Our acceptance is not in what we do, but, rather, in whose we are. "See what kind of love the Father has given to us, that we should be called children of God; and so we are" (1 John 3:1a). Prayerfully, we will be less resistant as we experience more and more of God's grace in our lives.

If we believe that we earned our standing before God, we will not know God or his love, and we will not pursue others with relentless devotion. But if we have experiential knowledge of God's love, we will have compassion for others and relentlessly love them. John's letter gives us some insight to our response to the Father's love: "Beloved, let us love one another, for love is from God, and whoever loves has been born of God and knows God. Anyone who does not love does not know God, because God is love. . . . Beloved, if God so loved us, we also ought to love one another" (1 John 4:7–8, 11).

Let Your Father Embrace You

When I was nineteen, I borrowed my dad's new Chevy Silverado truck to go to a year-end party at my college. My dad worked hard, and he always had an older "beater" truck to drive back and forth to work. This Chevy, however, was his first new truck. I believe taking his vehicle instead of mine (a small-sized 1974 Toyota truck) was God's sovereign protection of my life.

My two best friends accompanied me to the party. Eventually, however, we were kicked off campus when the police would not allow me to do donuts on the campus lawn. Buzzkill! They released us on the condition that we leave town immediately, and they followed us to the city limits. Driving home, I fell asleep and rammed into the back of a van parked on the side of the highway. I had to climb out of the truck's window, and an ambulance rushed me to the hospital with a hole in my lung (pneumothorax). They did an emergency procedure with no anesthesia and a lot of screaming pain, but I survived. However, I totaled my dad's new truck. If I had taken my small, aluminum-clad Toyota truck, I most likely would not have survived the impact. The worst thing about that experience was how my irresponsibility destroyed my dad's new truck. I was ashamed, embarrassed, and utterly worthy of his scorn. When my dad came to the hospital, I immediately expressed sorrow and humiliation for wrecking his new truck. My dad, not known for demonstrations of affection or many words, just bent over, hugged me, and whispered in my ear, "It's okay. You're my son, and that's all that matters."

In my disgrace, he reminded me of my identity as his son, and he extended undeserved forgiveness. He never brought it up again, even though my blatantly rebellious actions ruined his truck. I never paid the price for my indiscretion because he absorbed it completely. His recklessly extravagant grace opened up my heart to another Father with extravagant love. I experienced a complete spiritual transformation as a result and it serves as a basis for my leadership today.

I do not ever want to walk alone. The Father is walking with me by grace, and I am his beloved son in whom he is well pleased. The Father embraces me, and that reassures me when others reject me. As leaders, we can walk with God as sons or daughters who then demonstrate the Father's love. We cannot lead anyone without the Father's continual embrace.

Your Turn . . .

Prayer to Embrace the Father's Love

Lord, let me boast in you and not in any human accomplishment. I bear no great gifts except a heart to receive your love for me. Even in my carelessness, you run out to embrace me and welcome me back into your presence as your beloved child. You clothe me with your righteousness, and you desire to walk every step with me. Thank you that I can rest in your embrace.

Coaching Questions

1. In what ways have you struggled in your spiritual walk with God?
2. What calamity in your life led you to take decisive (or repentant) action?
3. How has an embrace of grace changed you?

4.
PLAN

Gospel-Shaped Leaders Design Their Lives with God's Purpose

> Desire that your life count for something great! Long for your life to have eternal significance. Want this! Don't coast through life without a passion.
>
> John Piper, *Don't Waste Your Life*

Self-awareness has three dynamics. The first is dying to self as a servant of Christ for the good of others (John 10:11). The second is walking with God when we are aware of our identity with our Father. The third dynamic, discussed in this chapter, is being aware of what we are to be and do as a servant who belongs to God. Our self-awareness prepares us to design our life with God's purpose.

Aristotle taught that each person's life has a purpose and that the aim of that person's life was to attain that purpose. As far back as I can remember, I have wanted my life to count for something. As a seven-year-old, I prayed to God that I would be a scientist and discover something helpful to others. As a ten-year-old, I envisioned being a preacher. Then as a teen, I turned my back on the Lord, stopped going to church, and had many dark, depressing, and purposeless days. I was self-obsessed and insecure. I rediscovered God and dedicated myself to ministry once again. But, unconsciously, I led people toward a project instead of a Person; a ministry instead of a Man. I thought growing a ministry was my purpose. As I experienced fruitfulness, I felt my purpose was leading a church to be back on mission.

I had a skewed view of glorifying God through ministry accomplishments. Interestingly, I realized the way that I could glorify God best was not by accomplishing anything. Rather, I realized God's purpose for me was giving my life for the development of church leaders and their families. I coauthored a book about shepherding leaders.[1] I spent ten years training church leaders on how to instill the gospel into others' lives. I recognized my purpose and calling to not be a player, but a coach.

In six days, God made the world and everything in it. He made male and female and gave them dominion over every living thing and instructed them to be fruitful and multiply (Genesis 1:26–28). God has a purpose for us. As the Westminster Shorter Catechism reminds us, "Man's chief end is to glorify God, and to enjoy him forever." Our divine Creator links his will with the Christian's purpose.

God created people as his image-bearers. We are to reflect the glory of God in everything we do regardless of circumstances. That means even if things go horribly wrong, your purpose is to glorify God. If ministry is successful, you glorify him. If it is not going well, you glorify him. Whether health, finances, family, or vocation are going well or tanking badly, the purpose of glorifying God does not change. As Jesus passed by a man blind from birth, his disciples asked him, "'Rabbi, who sinned, this man or his parents, that he was born blind?' Jesus answered, 'It was not that this man sinned, or his parents, but that the works of God might be displayed in him'" (John 9:2–3). That changed my perspective. I must glorify God with everything that happens, good or bad.

Fruitful leaders aren't just those who are abundantly gifted; they are those who know their life purpose is to glorify God and pursue it with passion. Jim Elliot was a missionary to Ecuador's Huaorani people. He said, "I seek not a long life, but a full one, like you, Lord Jesus." He died a martyr at the age of twenty-eight. His work among the Huaorani—those who killed him—continued long after his death. Jim would often quote Mark 8:35, "For whoever would save his life will lose it, but whoever loses his life for my sake and the gospel's will save it." Eternity is at stake and it is worth our best effort. Tertullian said, "The blood of the martyrs is the seed of the church."

I have had the opportunity to meet some of the most successful leaders in North America. Before meeting these extraordinary people, their brilliance, skills, and accomplishments intimidated me. However, after meeting these renowned authors, CEOs, businesspeople, professors, presidents of corporations, denominational leaders, entrepreneurs, politicians, inventors, and musicians, I discovered three common things about them. First, they are not as extraordinary as I had envisioned. Second, they understood their purpose for life. Third, they pursued it with uncommon passion. This revelation was eye-opening and encouraging to me. I thought they were some kind of superheroes unattainable by a mere mortal like me. Their humanness gave me hope to pursue something I thought was unreachable.

Their ordinary skill is only "extraordinary" for one reason: they passionately pursue their God-ordained purpose in life and refuse to make excuses about their inadequacies. Emotionally healthy leaders are aware of their strengths and confidently apply their skills to advance God's kingdom. They also recognize their weaknesses and allow others to lead where they are not as effective. Immature leaders insert their leadership even when they are not helpful, whereas emotionally mature leaders focus on their areas of strength. D. L. Moody described how he served God as "my human best, filled with the Holy Spirit."[2] That's the secret to fruitful leadership.

Martin Luther King Jr. inspired many people with his life. In 1967, in a speech to students in Philadelphia, King talked about building a life's purpose. He said, "If it falls your lot to be a street sweeper, sweep streets like Michelangelo painted pictures. Sweep streets like Beethoven composed music. . . . Sweep streets like Shakespeare wrote poetry. Sweep streets so well that all the hosts of heaven and earth will have to pause and say: Here lived a great street sweeper who swept his job well. . . . Be the best of whatever you are."[3] I agree with King that we should do the best we can regardless of the job. But I would also add that we can pioneer new ventures as God leads us. Discover how you will glorify God and don't hold back.

Jonathan Edwards said a person of ordinary abilities would accomplish more with enthusiasm and resolve than a person ten times more gifted without zeal and resolve.[4] Let's be careful, however, not to equate vocation with identity. *Who* we are is not based on *what* we do. If we confuse these things we make what social psychologists call a *fundamental attribution error.*[5] Our behavior or job do not define us. We wrongly attribute certain personality traits to people who are doctors, teachers, pastors, and politicians, to name a few. I believe we should do the best in every endeavor, but our success doesn't define us. Our vocation, heritage, education, ethnicity, and so forth, do not define us. God ascribes our worth through the work of Christ. He only asks that we glorify him, regardless of the outcome. This truth immensely affects how we will plan and approach our life.

Envision, Design, Execute, and Trust

How will we glorify God? We can't create our vision or base it on what others expect. We will become an emotional wreck trying to accomplish what God did not purpose for us. If we attempt to live up to others' expectations for our lives, we will fail every time. God's purpose for us is all that matters. I spoke to a pastor recently who experienced personal sorrow. On the other side of that dark time, he found his purpose. He figured out how he would glorify God and that brought peace to his restless soul.

> I am no longer interested in being a visionary leader. I am interested in shepherding the flock of God. I just want to preach, be with the people, visit them, care for them, be hospitable to the lost, etc. I don't have some watermark that I hope to hit. I just want to pastor those God gives me. It isn't particularly inspiring to young guys, which concerns me. I was that kind of leader when I was much younger. The Lord gave me a difficult season with my wife's health, which deeply drove home that I just wanted to pastor, love my family, and spend time with friends. Knowing the Lord and His people is enough.[6]

How about you? Can you remove all of the unrealistic visions of grandeur and concentrate for a moment on how you believe you can best glorify God? The first thing you have to do is envision God's purpose with clarity. In Numbers 13, the twelve spies return to Moses to report what they have discovered about the land of Canaan. They have found it to be unassailable even though it is flowing with milk and honey. They liken themselves to grasshoppers that would be destroyed by the inhabitants. Caleb, one of the spies, "quieted the people before Moses and said, 'Let us go up at once and occupy it, for we are well able to overcome it'" (Numbers 13:30). At that point, Caleb becomes a significant leader. He first quiets the negative chatter of those around him. Leaders must learn to mute the critics and naysayers to envision God's purpose for them. Leaders with quiet spirits are gifts to those they lead. Focus on quieting your soul and envisioning what God is calling you to be and do. You cannot purposefully design your life for that which you cannot see. Envision it with clarity.

Second, design or plan how you will accomplish God's purpose for you. Jesus says no builder builds a tower without first counting the cost, and no king goes to war without having a plan (Luke 14:28–32). You will rarely build or overcome anything without a plan. God is sovereign, and he alone controls outcomes, but we are not to presume on God by backing him into a corner with an empty battle plan (cf. Luke 4:12). Having no strategy is like saying, "Okay, God, you promised to watch over me and protect me, so I'm going to take this massive dose of poison to see your omnipotence." Presuming on God is not faith; it's foolishness. Make a plan and let God empower it and let him change it if he wills.

Third, execute the plan by faith. Take the idea that you believe God has led you and execute it. As my country singer friend, Mo Pitney, sang, "If you don't move your feet, you'll never dance if you don't take the chance."[7] Some leaders underthink, and some leaders overthink, producing analysis paralysis. Make the plan and then start dancing. It won't be perfect. But it will be utterly lost if you don't take the first step.

Fourth, trust God for the results and rest from your labors without replaying the outcome in your mind. You certainly evaluate your actions so that you can grow to become a skillful shepherd (Psalm 78:70–72), but you have to be careful of moving into self-loathing—the hidden side of pride. Trust God with the results. Paul says, "I planted, Apollos watered, but *God gave the growth*. So, neither he who plants nor he who waters is anything, *but only God who gives the growth*" (1 Corinthians 3:6–7, emphasis added).

Envision God's purpose for your life. Design a strategy to accomplish it. Execute the plan by faith, and then trust God with the outcome he desires.

Disabled and Determined

Terry Fox found his purpose in life and captivated the whole nation of Canada in the process. Fox ran 5,373 kilometers (3,224 miles) in 143 days (almost a marathon a day), but that is not what made him stand out from other long-distance runners. Fox ran on one natural leg and one prosthetic leg. He ran with his broken body to raise money for cancer research through his charity, Marathon of Hope. Cancer eventually took his life, but his cancer didn't cancel his cause. He had a lofty dream to raise $1 million for cancer research. Did his goal fall short due to his death? Thirty years later, the Marathon of Hope Foundation raised more than $600 million for cancer research, and his courage and passion continue to be a beacon of inspiration for all Canadians.

What is your calling in life? Are you pursuing it or avoiding it with a litany of excuses? As a one-legged man with cancer, Fox had the best excuse for not participating in a marathon. What reasons do you tend to give for not making your life count?

Jerry Traylor graduated several years ahead of me from the same high school. I remember him as the manager of our athletic teams. He always did his job with a smile and a pair of crutches. Jerry had ataxic cerebral palsy. In spite of that, he successfully ran 3,528 miles across the United States, from San Francisco to New York City. Jerry climbed the 14,115-foot Pike's Peak—one of the most imposing challenges an athlete can ever contemplate, much less someone with cerebral palsy—three different times. He competed in 35 marathons. Jerry died of cancer in 2018 at the age of 63. "When people say that I've overcome obstacles, I tell them that it's not true," Jerry said. "I tell them that I have learned to work within my limits and use what God has given me. There's nothing special about me."[8]

Most of us don't have just one leg, cancer, or cerebral palsy. What excuses will we set aside to pursue our passion? Excuses are easy. Leadership of self is difficult.

Narcissism Isn't a Leadership Style

I have worked alongside leaders who forgot the vital gospel principle of leaving their self-interests aside for others' good. When we become consumed with ourselves, the gospel has

little room to work through us. Narcissus, a Greek mytho-
logical figure, distinguished for his beauty, fell in love with
his reflection in the still waters of a spring, and killed himself
because he could not have himself. Some leaders are motivated by their self-glorifying success. It results in an excessive
ambition and drive and can result in narcissism—an epidemic
in our day. Narcissism is a personality trait encompassing
grandiosity, arrogance, self-absorption, entitlement, fragile
self-esteem, and hostility. Narcissistic leaders have grandiose
belief systems and leadership styles and are generally motivated by their need for power and admiration rather than
empathetic concern for the constituents and institutions they
lead.[9] I've witnessed several leaders self-destruct with narcissistic behaviors. Some believed they deserved sexual pleasure
outside of marriage. Some led with a bully mentality, uti-
lizing fear, shame, and false accusations as their weapons to
build a self-centered platform. But gospel-shaped leaders are
not celebrities, are not the center of attention, draw no attention to self, and are not boastful. Gospel-shaped leaders are
not climbing the ladder of success; they are busy shouldering
others up the ladder. Gospel-shaped leaders are not out for
themselves.

What do you need to be willing to leave? What is holding you back from pursuing the purpose God has placed in
your heart? Jesus tells a rich young man to sell his possessions
and give to the poor before following him. The young man
goes away sorrowful because he has great wealth (Matthew
19:21–22). Jesus doesn't generally ask others to give away their
possessions, but it is what held back this man from genuinely
trusting in Jesus for eternal life. He wouldn't leave his money
for Jesus. If you left your home, your job, or your friends,

would your life feel empty? Can you die to self? Jesus says, "If anyone comes to me and does not hate his own father and mother and wife and children and brothers and sisters, yes, and even his own life, he cannot be my disciple" (Luke 14:26). We will only discover and pursue our passion when our mission is not self-centered but God-glorifying. Paul describes the kinds of leaders for whom he had little patience: "For they all seek their own interests, not those of Jesus Christ" (Philippians 2:21). There is no room for hirelings who care nothing for the sheep, and there is no use for leaders who are more interested in their benefit above the good of the church they shepherd.

Follow God's Purpose for Your Life

When Jesus chooses his first disciples, he says to them, "Follow me, and I will make you fishers of [people]" (Matthew 4:19). God will give you a purpose if you follow him, and he will provide the just-in-time training that you need to follow him: "I will *make* [transform, shape, resource, enable] you fishers of [people]." The disciples immediately leave their nets, boats, and family and follow him (Matthew 4:20–22). That's a staggering response. Without hesitation, they leave their source of income, their occupation, their identity, their predictable and relatively safe lifestyle, and follow Jesus. Jesus gives them the vision to cease doing what they know—casting nets and gathering fish—and begin anew by casting a spiritual net and gathering people for the King.

Would we immediately leave our jobs (nets), our family (father), and our resources (boats) and follow him? Married friends of ours left a secure and significant ministry role, and a beautiful home in Nashville, and followed Jesus back to Canada, their homeland, to plant a church in Toronto, one of the largest and most diverse cities in North America. This couple said just considering the idea of uprooting their family was hard on them. But the more they sought God's will, the more precise the calling became. They believed God had a plan for Toronto, and that plan included them.

Sometimes people will try to convince you that you are mistaken about God's purpose for your life. Can you envision it? If you lack this vision, you will give up on your goal and settle for mediocrity and miss what God has in mind. Jesus, the Good Shepherd, is leading you to follow him. He is your focal point, and he will guide and equip you to care for his sheep.

My wife, Jeannie, traveled with me from Toronto, where we were living, to Denver to visit her dad. She passed out on the plane due to her kidney disease. Her health was so bad that doctors advised us to stay in Colorado. We lived in her dad's basement for eighteen months while she recovered. I commuted to Canada during the week and spent the week-ends in Colorado. In Colorado, the Lord graciously led us to start a church with a vision for reaching the "none and done." Forty percent of the people in that city indicated "none" on their census for their church affiliation while many others in the medium-sized town had given up on church but not on God. Only 9 percent of the city attended a Bible-believing church. We did not pursue a method; we pursued a call-ing. Our church-planting core group made an offer to buy a downtown facility that previously served as a bar and restau-rant. We had little money but an abundance of vision. It was a calling that we all pursued in obedience to Jesus. To our surprise, we were able to get a loan and raise enough money for a down payment. The upper floor of the facility that once served as a nightclub dance floor became our sanctuary. Every week, wanting our core group to see and feel the vision, I repeated it. Most of all, I wanted them to respond to Jesus, who was calling us to a humanly improbable adventure. When the members began taking their own initiative toward that vision, we knew they had embraced the vision with God-given passion. At a church gathering, a woman told me she used to sell drugs in the same room where I had just baptized her in our portable baptistry! Redemption happened in that 125-year-old former bar. It was as if God was telling me, "This was my purpose for this new church." Jeannie said that was the purpose for her illness, so a broken people could launch the only downtown church in that city.

You will inspire others when you know your purpose. Follow Jesus and he will lead and transform you, and renew your dreams as you passionately pursue as much of the vision as he reveals to you at the time.

Don't Quit

I don't want to end this chapter without addressing the discouragement that often accompanies our pursuit of a vision. We have to anticipate opposition and impediments if we have a vision. Our plans may not often (or ever) work out exactly as we envision or at the pace we expect. But if we receive a clear vision from God, it will carry us through setbacks.

Job refuses to give up on his vision to live for his Redeemer despite a series of devastating circumstances. He says to the Lord, "I know that you can do all things and that no purpose of yours can be thwarted" (Job 42:2). Nothing can prevent the purpose of God. Don't quit.

Daniel is a man of vision who courageously worships God even when doing so is punishable by being cast into a den of lions (Daniel 6:7, 10). His vision for God is more compelling than his fear of man. Daniel escapes the lions' den; his accusers do not. The lions crush the bones of his accusers when the king casts them into the same den (Daniel 6:24). Don't quit.

Nehemiah has a vision for rebuilding the wall around Jerusalem (Nehemiah 2:4–5, 11–18). He continues to build in spite of opposition (Nehemiah 4). The builders work with a tool in one hand, a weapon in the other, and a sword at their side (Nehemiah 4:17–18). Don't quit.

Overcoming discouragement begins when we resolve to glorify God regardless of circumstances. I have grown disillusioned when I focused on my challenges instead of my calling. We have to see his sovereign care, power, mission, and unseen guiding hand. He can give us a clear and compelling vision to pursue no matter what problems we encounter. But you have to be aware of those you are leading. Ray Ortlund told me his dad used to say, "If you are one step ahead, you are a leader. If you are two steps ahead, you are a visionary. But if you are three steps ahead, you are a martyr." Self-awareness is knowing where we are in comparison to those we are leading.

Some of you may still be stuck. You may feel that your window of opportunity is lost, or your life is not what you imagined it to be. Age, divorce, health issues, finances, education, marital status, and geography must not deter you from pursuing your purpose from this point forward. Paul says, "Forgetting what lies behind and straining forward to what lies ahead. I press on toward the goal for the prize of the upward call of God in Christ Jesus" (Philippians 3:13b–14).

Press on, leader. God can use you, an ordinary man or woman with failures, flaws, and fears (like me), if you understand your God-glorifying purpose in life and pursue it faithfully. It's not too late to "lead the life that the Lord has assigned to [you], and to which God has called [you]" (1 Corinthians 7:17). Don't quit.

Your Turn . . .

Prayer for a Life with Purpose

Lord, I give you my life for the sake of the gospel. Quiet my soul to follow your leading. I want to be and do what you desire. Help me to see it with clarity and help me to execute your plan for my life. The church belongs to you, Jesus, and by faith I am trusting the outcomes to you. I lay down my life for your sheep. Help me to persevere.

Coaching Questions

1. What purpose is God impressing on your heart to pursue?
2. What would it take to pursue your vision?
3. For whom can you lay down your life?
4. What have you always wanted to pursue but have been hesitant?

Part Two
Self-Management

You were taught, with regard to your former way of life,
to put off your old self, which is being corrupted by its
deceitful desires; to be made new in the attitude of your
minds; and to put on the new self, created to be like God in
true righteousness and holiness.

Ephesians 4:22–24 NIV

Self-Management. I am submitting my mind, will, and emotions to the desires of the Spirit and not to the desires of the flesh (Galatians 5:16–26). The gospel is continually shaping me (Philippians 1:27) through the power of the Spirit (Romans 8:4–11). I am confessing my sins and acknowledging my weaknesses (1 John 1:7–9). I am striving for holiness and the renewing of my mind that leads to a transformed life (Romans 12:1–2). With my hope in Jesus, I'm patient in hardships and constant in prayer (Romans 12:12).

5.
STAND

Gospel-Shaped Leaders
Pursue Integrity

*Integrity is the best of all protectors . . . since we cannot be
more secure than when fortified by a good conscience.*

John Calvin, *Commentary on Daniel*

I sat stunned in the study of the first church where I served
as lead pastor. Two deacons questioned me for purchas-
ing janitorial supplies without their approval when in fact
the church had formally approved the budget for custodial
supplies. Who could argue about cleaning a facility used six
days a week? Even so, I found myself defending my character over toilet paper and air freshener. This church that we
were replanting was finally out of debt, including the mort-
gage. Regardless, these two deacons, who had experienced
much leaner years, accused me of buying too many trashcan
liners. The unexpected confrontation made me feel rejected
and I had an emotional collapse when they left. I knew at the
time that it only takes two people to destroy the reputation
of a church leader—one to say it and another to believe it.
In response to this perceived attack, instead of training the
deacons on financial procedures for a church, I turned every
financial decision over to them. I drove them and me silly

with multiple purchase-order requests. They grew more controlling and I grew more resentful. It wasn't a gospel-shaped course of action.

Integrity is the most critical asset of a church leader. Without integrity, leaders are useless and, in fact, toxic. Integrity means wholeness, completeness, soundness. The lack of integrity is one of the results of being under the power of sin. Only Jesus can restore wholeness by breaking the power of sin through his death and resurrection. Jesus tells us that if anyone is in Christ Jesus, he is a new creation (2 Corinthians 5:17). Jesus alone is our integrity. Paul tells believers that his battle with integrity has not been won by sheer discipline, but only through Jesus Christ: "For I do not understand my own actions. For I do not do what I want, but I do the very thing I hate. . . . Wretched man that I am! Who will deliver me from this body of death? Thanks be to God through Jesus Christ our Lord!" (Romans 7:15, 24–25a).

Regarding the money collected from the Macedonian church, the apostle Paul repeatedly emphasizes the integrity of the leaders who would be carrying out the distribution. He says they were taking great pains toward integrity "so that no one should blame us about this generous gift that is being administered by us, for we aim at what is honorable not only in the Lord's sight *but also in the sight of man*" (2 Corinthians 8:20–21, emphasis added). We must be above the accusation of others and avoid the appearance of evil (1 Thessalonians 5:22). Paul further points out that those he was sending had been "often tested and found earnest in many matters" (2 Corinthians 8:22). If leaders are negligent in one area, they will likely compromise other matters. Integrity cannot be assumed; it must be tested often. J. C. Ryle, the first Anglican bishop of Liverpool, reminded us, "You may be very sure men fall in private long before they fall in public."[1]

I'm pained every time someone accuses a church leader of financial, moral, sexual, or disqualifying actions. It hurts for two reasons. First, it brings reproach on the integrity of God's family. Second, it hurts because I know every church leader is vulnerable to sin's effects. We are all only a step away from moral catastrophe. Acknowledging this reality can save us from years of heartache. When we think we're above temptation, we are most susceptible. We have to admit that sin crouches at the local church's door, and it desires to rule over every leader (Genesis 4:7).

Paul warns leaders, "Brothers, if anyone is caught in any transgression, you who are spiritual should restore him in a spirit of gentleness. *Keep watch on yourself, lest you too be tempted*" (Galatians 6:1, emphasis added). Gospel-shaped leaders are aware of their actions, emotions, and moods. In short, they exercise the second dimension of emotional intelligence: self-management. *Self*-management is a bit of a misnomer because we can only manage self in a community with others. Self-management is the ability to submit mind, will, and emotions to the desires of the Spirit and not to the desires of the flesh (Galatians 5:16–26). Self-managed leaders allow the gospel to continually shape them (Philippians 1:27) through the power of the Spirit (Romans 8:4–11) as they confess their sins and acknowledge their weaknesses (1 John 1:7–9). Self-managed leaders strive for holiness and the renewing of their minds that leads to transformed lives (Romans 12:1–2). Self-managed leaders confess their sins to one another and pray for one another, that they may be healed (James 5:16).

Examining Paul's list of qualifications for church leadership (1 Timothy 3:1–13; Titus 1:5–9), we find an ability to teach as the only actual skill. All the other church leadership qualifications are characterized by integrity; they are based on character. The first qualification found in both lists in 1 Timothy 3:2 and Titus 1:6 is "above reproach," which means filled with integrity and serves as the foundation for all other qualifications. The lists differ slightly, but above reproach is first on both lists. Although this passage addresses the criteria for an elder, it serves as the character standard for which all church leaders should strive. A leader with integrity will adhere to moral, ethical, and biblical principles with unflappable discipline and honest self-evaluation—not just for meaningful ministry to others, but also for healthy leadership of self.

When we consistently compromise integrity, we dive headfirst into an extremely steep, long, unstoppable moral Slip 'N Slide that will ultimately land in a pool of brokenness and shame. Ray Ortlund said, "Jesus isn't impressed with our reputations. What matters to Him is our integrity. So He is willing, if we force Him by our excuses and delays, to embarrass us until we come clean before Him and others. He doesn't relish it. But He's willing. Because our integrity matters most."[2] Embarrassment does not always require public exposure. Hopefully, a single broken relationship or sinful act can trigger repentance. Sin brings consequences, and if we are leaders, it affects us and those around us. Leaders may not intend to hurt others, but a leader's sin always hurts others. A fallen leader who refuses to repent and respond with integrity will further hurt the body of Christ.

The Danger of Success

I become concerned when young leaders experience disproportionate ministry accomplishments. I saw rapid success happen to a few. Their achievements changed their relationships with people. They began to heap unsustainable expectations on others while obscuring their failures behind their accomplishments. They manipulated people with force and made unverified accusations from their positions of unrestrained power. They would attack the weak and then discredit them because of their weaknesses.

I confronted one leader who lied in a sermon. He laughed and said, "I know it was a lie, but it made them laugh, didn't it?" His church disciplined him five years later for character reasons and he left. Many people who have ministered close to fallen leaders knew something was amiss. But their value to the organization and their fear of reprisal by the powerful leaders, made them look the other way.

"Success has made failures of many men," *New York Post* columnist Cindy Adams quipped. You can measure integrity with more accuracy when a person experiences success than when they experience failure. A gospel-shaped leader cannot pine after or abuse power. Power without character results in chaos.

Leaders must be careful not to exploit their position of power, no matter how much or how little they possess. Every leader in the church has responsibilities and rights in the body. The self-managed leader is increasingly gentle in proportion to their biblical authority.

Ministry leaders need to be known. We can't simulate community or let our busy schedules prevent us from real biblical relationships where we are known at the deepest level.

The word *integrity* comes from the Latin word *integer*, which means wholeness. An integer is also a math term that means a whole number in contrast to a fraction. In reality, others only know a fraction of our life, but we must intentionally move closer to being wholly known. A leader who is only partly known is vulnerable to failure. A gospel-shaped leader will seek to be known. This doesn't mean every single person needs to know about every nook and cranny of our life, but it should concern us if no one truly knows us.

Becoming proud of success is not isolated to the gifted person. Institutional pride often affects all leaders in a thriving ministry. And this temptation isn't isolated to mega-churches but can affect small- and medium-sized churches just as easily. Here are some indicators of corporate pride:

- We are the best in the city.
- We have the inside track on ministry.
- We produce our own superior materials.
- We alone have God's blessing.
- We rely on our strategies more than the Spirit.

Sin Management

Hiding sin is not self-management, it is self-deception. We cannot hide or excuse sin and hope others won't discover it. We don't have to remain in shame and guilt. We can turn through repentance and receive cleansing and renewal. David began to lead others (Psalm 51:13) after he had a clean heart (Psalm 51:1–12). Without a clear conscience, we cannot lead others with discernible power.

The speed of sin's descent increases exponentially over time and grows in power with every compromise. A person who lacks integrity will believe they are in control and will try to navigate the twists and turns even as the rate of descent increases. A person who repeatedly compromises their integrity will crash unless they repent. A crocodile cannot be a family pet, nor can sin be tamed. James gives us the futile outcome of sin management: "But each person is tempted when he is lured and enticed by his own desire. Then desire when it has conceived gives birth to sin, and sin when it is fully grown, brings forth death" (James 1:14–15).

Satan is a roaring lion seeking someone to devour (1 Peter 5:8)—especially leaders. Billy Graham said, "The greatest roadblock to Satan's work is the Christian who, above all else, lives for God, walks with integrity, is filled with the Spirit, and is obedient to God's truth."[3]

Stop the Descent

The good news is that it is never too late to stop the descent. It requires, however, full confession and repentance. The only way to stop the decline is to walk in the light:

> If we say we have fellowship with him while we walk in darkness, we lie and do not practice the truth. But if we walk in the light, as he is in the light, we have fellowship with one another, and the blood of Jesus his Son cleanses us from all sin. If we say we have no sin, we deceive ourselves, and the truth is not in us. If we confess our sins, he is faithful and just to forgive us our sins and to cleanse us from all unrighteousness. If we say we have not sinned, we make him a liar, and his word is not in us. (1 John 1:6–10)

The American Automobile Association (AAA) comes to your rescue when you have car trouble. I once accidentally left my car in neutral on a hill. When I got out and closed the door, I helplessly watched as it rolled down the hill and into a ditch. I called AAA who came and pulled my car out.

Another AAA acronym is what we need when our life breaks down: (1) admit your sin; (2) accept God's forgiveness; and (3) act like a child of God.

1. *Admit* your sin. Stop lying to yourself and stop living in the darkness. Tell God what he already knows. This rich source of healing is available to us regardless of the extent of our sin. He does not push us away when we confess; he embraces us even tighter. Pause and reflect on that truth. He does not respond like a man. God is the "Holy One in [our] midst and . . . will not come in wrath (Hosea 11:9b).

2. *Accept* God's forgiveness. He is faithful to his promises to forgive and cleanse us. Our penalty is not only erased, but its claim on us is eradicated. The filth of our sin no longer identifies us. *If* we confess our sins, it triggers God's forgiveness and cleansing (1 John 1:9).

3. *Act* in line with our identity as cleansed and forgiven children of God. In Christ, our forgiveness and cleansing produce our identity, and that identity fosters a gospel-transformed life. Both forgiveness and cleansing are necessary for our identity, and it informs our subsequent actions. Self-condemnation is treating our sin in a self-centered way instead of a gospel-centered way where Jesus, the perfect one who loves us, forgives our sins and cleanses us.

Church leaders must live with integrity in every area of their life. We have no secret compartments. Gospel-shaped leaders address inconsistencies by admitting sin, accepting forgiveness, and acting in line with their identity. Integrity affects our life and others' lives.

What's the Worst Thing That Can Happen?

At a training session for church leaders, I asked them to write down the effect their worst sin would have on their life if it were not put to death through the Spirit's power. One by one, the leaders imagined outcomes of tragedy, loss, brokenness, and shame that could happen in their lives. After that sobering exercise, I asked the participants how they could apply the gospel to that sin. Collectively, they came up with the answer that if they viewed themselves as God's children who were dearly beloved, they would be more prone to act accordingly. This truth about God produces a resultant action. Young people who believe a lie that they are unloved will allow themselves to be treated inappropriately (resultant effect). You are forgiven fully (a truth you can believe), and you can act in a cleansed and renewed manner (resultant action). If we only focus on the action, we act according to moralism or legalism. If we only focus on the truth without subsequent steps, we may live in a sinful or lewd manner. The gospel calls for us to live in line with the good news. Because the Lord cleanses, loves, forgives, and redeems, we act with integrity.

"For every look at yourself, take ten looks at Christ," said Scottish pastor Robert Murray McCheyne. McCheyne was not suggesting turning a blind eye to our sin. Here is the full context:

> The heart is deceitful above all things, and desperately wicked: who can know it? (Jer. 17:9). Learn

much of the Lord Jesus. For every look at yourself, take ten looks at Christ. He is altogether lovely. Such infinite majesty, and yet such meekness and grace, and all for sinners, even the chief! Live much in the smiles of God. Bask in his beams. Feel his all-seeing eye settled on you in love, and repose in his almighty arms. . . . Let your soul be filled with a heart-ravishing sense of the sweetness and excellency of Christ and all that is in Him. Let the Holy Spirit fill every chamber of your heart; and so there will be no room for folly, or the world, or Satan, or the flesh.[4]

Believing a lie leads to wrong actions while believing a truth leads to the right actions.

Actions to Take

I suggest believing the following five practical truths that result in a ministry characterized by integrity.

Own Your Misspoken Words, Failures, and Mistakes

Admitting wrong will not decrease your influence, but rather increase it. You need the gospel, and you will need to show how to accept when you are wrong humbly and take responsibility for your actions. It is incongruous to proclaim the gospel and hide your inadequacies. The gospel brings reconciliation between our unholy lives and a holy God. A leader who lets others see their weaknesses emboldens the strength found in the gospel. Conversely, a leader who hides their flaws creates a dependency on an individual. When self-dependent leaders fail—and they will—the organizations will fail. When gospel-shaped leaders fail—and they will—their admission of wrong will strengthen the organization.

Stay Honest with All People

Stay honest regardless of the person's position in the church structure. Nobody is above accountability. Learn to address concerns quickly, even if it is uncomfortable for you. Paul Tripp suggests conflicts can be resolved in a redemptive way by saying the right thing at the right moment and with the right spirit.[5]

Integrity is living a transparent life, displaying honesty and trustworthiness. The relationship between integrity and trust is indispensable. Trust is the glue that bonds people, processes, and environments, and ensures long-term success. Transparent leaders live their values. Transparency opens the door to trust among those we lead. Gospel-shaped leaders openly admit their mistakes and confront unethical behavior in others rather than turn a blind eye.

Integrity is not emotional nudity. It is practicing authenticity and honesty while admitting need. If we do not have anything to hide, our integrity unshackles our insecurities with others. If we have something to hide, we will continuously be on guard, defensive, cynical, and worried others will expose us. A leader with integrity admits they are in constant need of the redeeming work of the gospel.

Expect to Be Misunderstood

You will have your motives misjudged, and your actions or inactions misinterpreted. You mean to say something one way, and others will take it in quite a different light. The apostle Paul faces questions about his integrity with the Corinthian church:

"Was I vacillating when I wanted to do this? Do I make my plans according to the flesh, ready to say 'Yes, yes' and 'No, no' at the same time?" (2 Corinthians 1:17). They questioned his actions and motives. People will repeatedly evaluate a leader's life, words, and decisions. It is natural to get defensive in this situation, but you must resist blaming others for the sake of the gospel. Christ did not act without his people in mind. The reproaches of others fell upon his shoulders (Romans 15:3).

Allow God to Vindicate You

When others falsely accuse you, rest in God's sovereign timing. You don't have to vindicate yourself (1 Peter 3:16–17). A Christian leader lied about me to others. I chose not to launch a counterattack, even though many people advised me to defend myself. One lawyer friend even offered to file a lawsuit on my behalf. I chose to let God deal with this person. It wasn't easy, but it was right. King David associates vindication with integrity: "The LORD judges the peoples; judge me, O LORD, according to my righteousness and according to the integrity that is in me" (Psalm 7:8). "Vindicate me, O LORD, for I have walked in my integrity, and I have trusted in the LORD without wavering" (Psalm 26:1).

Joseph served in the Egyptian household of Potiphar. When Joseph refused the advances of Potiphar's wife (Genesis 39), she lied about him, and he was thrown into prison. But the Lord was with Joseph in prison. Eventually, Joseph was vindicated, released, and rose to become second in command in Egypt (Genesis 41:37ff.). Later when his brothers who had sold him into slavery became afraid that Joseph would take vengeance on them for what they had done to him, Joseph said to them: "As for you, you meant evil against me, but God meant it for good, to bring it about that many people should be kept alive, as they are today" (Genesis 50:20). God may be preparing to use your most painful experiences for his good.

Flee Sin and Pursue Godliness

"Flee youthful passions and pursue righteousness, faith, love, and peace" (2 Timothy 2:22). We like to think that we can fight temptation and stand firm against the Devil. But Paul tells Timothy to *flee* sin and *pursue* godliness. Run from temptations to do wrong and run to opportunities to do right. Integrity requires simultaneous efforts. John Stott warned us about hanging around sin's company:

> True, we are also told to withstand the devil, so that he may flee from us. But we are to recognize sin as something dangerous to the soul. We are not to come to terms with it, or even negotiate with it. We are not to linger in its presence like Lot in Sodom. On the contrary, we are to get as far away from it as possible as quickly as possible. Like Joseph, when Potiphar's wife tried to seduce him, we are to take to our heels and run.[6]

The Other Side of Integrity

Integrity means living a whole and pure life before the Lord and others. It also means being faithful with the gifts entrusted to you. In Jesus's parable of the talents (Matthew 25:14ff.), the master entrusts gifts to servants, and they are instructed to multiply them for master's benefit. Each servant receives a different portion, but the reward is potentially the same. The master judges the servants not by the amount of return, but by faithfulness with the gifts. Investing the resources that the master entrusts to us will result in a reward; wasting them will result in a loss (Matthew 25:26, 30). God calls you to pursue integrity with your life and ministry.

You must commit to integrity for the sake of your soul and the people God entrusts to your care. Can you be trusted by your family, friends, coworkers, and church members? Are you reliable and dependable? Do you admit when you have failed, or do you make excuses and blame others?

For a church leader, integrity is not optional. You either have it and pursue it continually, or you must, out of reverence for the bride of Christ, step out of church leadership at least for a season.

Jesus is one we can depend on; he is one with integrity. Paul says of Jesus, "I am sure of this, that he who began a good work in you will bring it to completion on the day of Jesus Christ" (Philippians 1:6). The gospel is rooted in the integrity of Jesus to accomplish what he said he would. Jesus is a Savior who will always prove faithful; a friend whose words will never prove false. Jesus can be trusted fully—always.

In the opening paragraph when I turned over the church's daily financial decisions to two deacons, I did not handle it with maturity. My actions were defensible; I was doing what was honorable in God's sight. But I needed to do what was honorable in the sight of men too (2 Corinthians 8:20–21). I even asked if they wanted to inspect the inventory and they refused. But I didn't tell them how their attacks made me feel and how dangerous their unsubstantiated questions of integrity were to the advance of the gospel for that church. I wasn't patient or prayerful in responding to this attack (Romans 12:12).

Instead, I was passive aggressive. If I had it to do over, I would have received their accusations, prayed with them, and then brought the issue to the entire board to decide how we handle budgeted expenditures. Their accusations were shrouded in darkness and I should have brought them to the light. Instead, I allowed their accusations to dishearten me and affect my relationship with the entire board.

Your Turn . . .

Prayer for Wholeness

Lord, I am incomplete without you. I don't always understand why I think and do the things I do. Thank you for being my deliverer from the failings of my wretched body. Help me walk in the light with you and with others. Help me to confess my sins in the moment they occur. When my heart is deceitful, may I trust in your Word and do the right thing. Keep me from wickedness and empower me to run away from it as fast as possible. Let me lead with integrity at all times.

Coaching Questions

1. Look at the list of qualifications in 1 Timothy 3 and Titus 1. What characteristics would you like to strengthen?
2. Who knows you well enough to ensure integrity in your life?
3. Look over the five actions to take. What action can you take today?

6.
LEARN

Gospel-Shaped Leaders
Explore New Ideas

Burning hearts are not nourished by empty heads.

R. C. Sproul

Pastor Lawrence served a local church for fourteen years as senior pastor. He experienced much growth in the ministry. He led the church to build two beautiful buildings: a sanctuary and an educational building. He earned respect among his peers and was well-liked. He had self-confidence and charisma. But he stalled in his fourteenth year. He wouldn't budge from what worked a decade earlier. He, the staff, and the congregation grew in their frustration. He resigned one Sunday morning without warning. Pastor Lawrence lacked a vital leadership skill: learning agility.

Learning agility is "the willingness and ability to learn from experience, and subsequently apply that learning to perform successfully under new or first-time conditions."[1] The church must proclaim the gospel, observe the sacraments, equip the saints, and exercise church discipline through biblically-qualified leaders. Beyond that, there is a lot of flexibility and we should remain open to new ideas to proclaim the gospel.

The degree of learning agility that a person has can mean the difference between being effective and fading away in times of crisis, transition, or stress. Agility is vital to managing and thriving in a typical church when change is required. Organizational change can be an emotional experience. Leadership is crucial when people go through changes. Paul expressed the role of a learning leader in disciplining others: "What you have *learned* and *received* and *heard* and *seen* in me—practice these things, and the God of peace will be with you" (Philippians 4:9, emphasis added).

Learning agility falls under our quadrant of self-management. Self-management includes submitting mind, will, and emotions to the desires of the Spirit so the gospel shapes the leader through the power of the Spirit. This leader does not hide weaknesses or make excuses, but leans on Jesus to shepherd the church through many people. Learning agile leaders do not live in the past but are renewing their minds with Christ's mind. "You were taught, with regard to your former way of life, to put off your old self, which is being corrupted by its deceitful desires; *to be made new in the attitude of your minds; and to put on the new self, created to be like God in true righteousness and holiness*" (Ephesians 4:22–24 NIV, emphasis added).

Leaders with a posture to learn can quickly grasp new insights and understandings, and make the necessary adaptations in life and work. Complex problems fascinate and intrigue leaders with a disposition to learning. Challenges attract and interest them. Agility isn't just another tool for your leadership toolbox. It's the master competency necessary for sustained success in today's uncertain future.[2] Learning is a major component of a follower of God. The psalmist says, "Make me to know your ways, O Lord; teach me your paths. Lead me in your truth and teach me, for you are the God of my salvation; for you I wait all the day long" (Psalm 25:4–5). Solomon says, "The fear of the Lord is the beginning of knowledge; *fools despise wisdom and instruction*" (Proverbs 1:7, emphasis added). It is foolish to stop learning more about the Lord and his work.

Mark Reynolds serves as vice president of leadership development at Redeemer City to City in New York City. He told me research does not explicitly describe learning agility as a competency; however, he believes that learning agility is the essential skill after godliness and entrepreneurial zeal (passion for people). He believes that it is even more critical in densely populated areas. He told me how Pastor Jon Tyson, an Australian-born church planter in New York City, moved his church from being one church in eleven neighborhoods to being eleven autonomous churches.[3] He did this without losing his church. He was agile enough to learn what worked and what didn't, and he led his whole church to adopt a new model. That risk took a lot of faith and a high degree of biblical wisdom. Reynolds posits that learning agility is not optional but essential for high-level leaders.[4]

The COVID-19 pandemic revealed which leaders could flex, adapt, and learn new ways of contributing to an organization's goals. The temporary closing of businesses also demonstrated which patrons could adapt to new realities. When the coronavirus pandemic forced restaurants to close, BJ's Restaurant and Bar in Mingus, Texas, turned their parking lot into a drive-in theater and offered carhop dining services.[5] They learned a new way to face a potential economic crisis. Ministries also had to adapt drastically. No longer could churches meet in person, and they had to quickly find new ways of connecting and serving their faith communities. It was a real test of leadership. Some church leaders responded swiftly and connected to their congregants. Others responded slowly and lost some momentum. Every church (and most businesses) experienced a dramatic change. Many discovered innovative ways to serve the body.

Four Characteristics of Learning Agility

Learning agility, as we have learned, is the competency to quickly understand a new concept or adapt to a new method and apply it effectively to a different context. Agile leaders refuse to accept current modes of operation if they impede future organizational growth. They are able to see a better way to accomplish a goal, build a new model—often with a team—and compel others to take advantage of it.

First, the person with learning agility is a *change-maker*. A change-maker is innovative for others' good. They identify a need and then evaluate new ideas and practices to meet that need. This person usually is a quick learner and is willing to try new things to benefit others. Change-makers are curious about how things work, and they explore how to make them better with relentless passion.

Jesus was the ultimate change-maker. He approached fishers, tax collectors, and even Zacchaeus in a tree. He invited all of them to set aside their agendas for life and follow him. Jesus asks someone to follow him twenty-two times throughout the Gospels. Jesus offers a better experience for those who would receive his wisdom and instruction.

Change-makers are necessary for the survival of a ministry. Conformists are unlikely to turn an organization around. Research indicates that your class valedictorian likely has a good job and is stable but does not change the world.[6] Playing according to the rules doesn't typically generate success. A study of over seven hundred American millionaires showed their average college GPA was a meager 2.9.[7] For every underachieving college student, this might be encouraging! The church needs change-making leaders. Change-makers lead the body to make changes *together*.

The second characteristic of a person with learning agility is that they are *people-initiators*. Learners have to make themselves vulnerable to new relationships and diverse experiences. They are always expanding their networks to learn how to further the gospel. People like this act friendly and extroverted, although, like me, it may only be functional extroversion to accomplish a task or learn a new trait. People-initiators draw from others' opinions and solicit their input. Jesus crosses racial and gender barriers to talk with the Samaritan woman at the well (John 4). Jesus initiates the conversation by asking for a drink. He then proceeds to tell her about the water of life that would quench her thirst forever. Leaders learn by listening, which often results in influential leadership.

I hesitate initiating conversations with people that I do not know. My pastor friend, Mario, is great at this. I was amazed at the number of neighbors attending his block party with whom he had built meaningful relationships in the short time he had lived there. And it wasn't just his neighborhood, because everywhere I went with him, he knew people and they seemed to be his best friend. He fearlessly initiates relationships, and people respond. Leadership agility is contagious, and it inspires people to think and act differently.

My wife and I moved into a subdivision of newly constructed homes. Since we were the first couple in the neighborhood, we took it upon ourselves to welcome all new residents as they moved in. We invited everyone to a neighborhood block party, and it kicked off a neighborhood of friends as I've never seen before. We have monthly parties, and every single day neighbors interact with each other. I know every resident by name, their kids, and all of the dogs. I ignore the cats, but so would Jesus, I suspect. I learned from Mario's example and discovered the joy of being a people-initiator.

Third, the person with learning agility is a *risk-taker*. Learning happens when you step outside of your comfort zone. Are you willing to pursue new relationships and new adventures? We encounter a lot of uncomfortable situations, but nothing will change if we merely complain about our condition. Leaders have to take a risk personally and organizationally.

A risk-taker will proactively explore new pathways, challenge norms and assumptions, and pose new ideas. Risk-takers intentionally create new opportunities for themselves and others. Leaders take risks—not unreasonable risks, but calculated risks with data, the teaching of the Holy Spirit (John 14:26), and biblical wisdom. If we rely on past successes, it stunts risk-taking endeavors. Being successful in one context doesn't necessarily translate into success in another. In fact, without learning agility, recent success leads to future failure for those unwilling to learn new techniques and skills.

Jesus didn't play it safe. He could have compromised when the religious and political leaders questioned him. If Jesus had been neutral, he would have had to abort his mission. Sometimes we either please God or people. When Jesus says, "It is the Spirit who gives life; the flesh is no help at all" and "no one can come to me unless it is granted by the Father," many of his disciples turned back and no longer walked with him (John 6:63–66). Jesus was not trying to build a local crowd. He was forming a committed core to start a revolution in the world. Perhaps the riskiest thing Jesus does is entrust us with his mission (John 17:18; 20:21). Christ takes away the ultimate risk, not by promising success in this world, but by promising us his peace amid trouble (John 16:33).

Learning-agile people are, fourth, *problem-solvers* who are calm in the face of challenges. They approach problems with a relentless can-do attitude and handle failures and set-backs with healthy fortitude. Sometimes problem-solvers will bounce back from a negative circumstance better than before. They can learn from experiences—positive or negative. Their responses to failure are what set these types of leaders apart from others.

Ray Ortlund Jr. faced a devastating setback at a pres-tigious church and subsequently started a new church in Nashville at the age of fifty-eight. This new church learned from all of the bad experiences and became the healthiest church I have personally experienced. They kept their gospel doctrine and added an equally valued emphasis on gospel cul-ture.[8] Church leaders must adapt to new people, procedures, places, and projects. When problems invariably arise in the church, the leaders must remain present and engaged, listen well, and stay connected to our problem-solving Lord. "One of the most reliable indicators and predictors of true lead-ership is an individual's ability to find meaning in negative events and learn from even the most trying circumstances."[9] Sometimes the most traumatic and unplanned events catapult us into beautiful discoveries about ourselves, our work, and our Savior.

Jesus has been teaching a large crowd all day (Mark 6:30–44). It is late and they are in a desolate location. The disciples disconnect from the heart of Jesus and ask him to send the people away to get food. Jesus the problem-solver takes charge and tells the perplexed disciples to feed the crowd of some fifteen thousand (five thousand men plus women and children) from the five loaves and two fish they come up with. Jesus organizes the crowd and the disciples distribute the food. Everyone is satisfied and they collect twelve baskets of leftovers. Problem–solving church teams can utilize systems and finances, but first and foremost, they must also have faith and compassion for those they lead (Mark 6:34–41).

Learning Agility in the Church

The Christian life begins with learning—learning the gospel.[10] The pastors, staff, officers, and members of the church must thoroughly devote themselves to learning about God the Father, God the Son, and God the Holy Spirit. Paul asks a redundant question, "How are they to believe in him of whom they have never heard?" (Romans 10:14b). Belief in the accomplished work of Christ begins with knowledge about him. God gives believers "the Spirit of wisdom and of revelation in the knowledge of him" (Ephesians 1:17b). At the base level, a disciple of Jesus is a learner and pupil of Jesus. They are learners (Greek, *mathetes*), devoted to learn (Greek, *manthano*), and striving to become a scholar (Latin, *discipulus*). The word *disciple* is found in the Gospels and Acts and always means the pupil or learner of someone.

One cannot be a true disciple of Jesus without learning about him. So, the Christian church depends on its leaders' openness to explore new ways to guide the flock to green pastures and still waters.

Gospel-shaped leaders never settle for convenient and comfortable. They labor to explore new ideas for the good of their brothers and sisters. We cannot stop learning. When we get older and cannot fight and labor in the Lord's field with the same physical intensity, we can fight to train young people to lead the church.

Leaders who become idle in their pursuit of new ideas to advance the church need to repent or resign. Idleness is the sin of burying a talent in the ground rather than investing it fruitfully. God entrusts leaders with an assignment to multiply God's kingdom. Jesus commends the one who faithfully invests while he condemns the slothful one (Matthew 25:14–30).

I knew a senior pastor who always complained about how busy he was and how hard the ministry was. His fatigued spiritual life depressed me as a young pastor. He eventually left the ministry and remained bitter at the church. D. L. Moody told the servants who thought they would perish from overwork in the church, "Something's amiss, good friends! There's [nothing] so restorative and health-giving as labor in the Lord!"[11] Leaders need to show others in the congregation how to labor for the Lord, which includes a regular rhythm of resting. There is joy in learning about God and telling others about him.

Renewing the Mind

We can only lead another person toward transformation when our renewed mind is an expression of our spiritual worship.

Paul tells the church at Rome, "I appeal to you, therefore, brothers, by the mercies of God, to present your bodies as a living sacrifice, holy and acceptable to God, which is your spiritual worship. Do not be conformed to this world, but be transformed by the *renewal of your mind*, that by testing you may discern what is the will of God, what is good and acceptable and perfect" (Roman 12:1–2, emphasis added).

R. C. Sproul reminds us, "Christianity is a faith of both mind and heart. God does not call us to surrender our rational faculties when we trust His Son; rather, it is only in serving Him that we use our minds as He created them."[12] We are leading the church toward Christ, in what is the good, acceptable, and perfect will of God, when our minds and hearts are prone to continuous learning—starting with Christ.

Keep Learning

In the opening paragraph, I mentioned Pastor Lawrence's sad resignation. I served as a youth pastor for Pastor John many years ago. He opened my eyes to the concept of staying true to the gospel while pursuing new ways of ministry. He allowed us to start a second youth group in the church aimed primarily at street kids who hadn't been in church. I used basketball and relationships as a bridge to introduce them to Jesus. My wife and I accepted kids coming from broken homes into our lives and they responded to our gospel-shaped love. This unconventional group eclipsed the traditional group in size and their passion and newfound faith spurred the church kids to a renewed commitment and zeal for the gospel's ability to reach teenagers who were different from them.

You can despise wisdom and instruction for new ideas, or you can take a chance and befriend unloved sinners in your community in need of Jesus. Jesus said, "Go and learn what this means, 'I desire mercy, and not sacrifice.' For I came not to call the righteous, but *sinners*" (Matthew 9:13, emphasis added).

Learning about God and his church never ends and never grows old. Lead the way forward as agile leaders who invest in the next generation.

Your Turn . . .

Prayer for a Learning Spirit

Lord, give me a heart and mind that long to know your ways and your truth. Renew my mind through the teaching of the Holy Spirit, the Helper. Use what I learn to be an example for others. Your Word is a lamp unto my feet and a light unto my path. Teach me, Lord, and lead me, for you are the God of my salvation.

Coaching Questions

1. How vital is learning agility among church leaders?
2. Which of the four characteristics of learning agility do you demonstrate well, and which need work?
3. What do you need to do to become a better learner of Jesus?

7.
REST

Gospel-Shaped Leaders Commit to Sabbath

Rest time is not waste time. It is economy to gather
fresh strength . . . a little pause prepares the mind for
greater service in the good cause. . . . It is wisdom to take
occasional furlough. In the long run, we shall do more by
sometimes doing less.

C. H. Spurgeon

A rested leader makes deposits to others while a restless
leader makes withdrawals. Paraphrasing the ancient
Roman poet Lucan, Spurgeon said, "See thou twist not the
rope so hard that it break."[1] In ministry, I brought stress to
my life and everyone around me because I wanted to succeed
at all costs. I worked incessantly to achieve, and my rope was
twisted, stretched, and frayed. It affected my ability to lead
those who weren't as driven as I was. Success was my idol, and
this idol didn't allow rest. I learned to work hard from both
of my parents. My dad worked a job until he turned ninety
years old. God ordained humans to work. It is his plan, and
it is good. But I worked hard to prove my worth. Outside of
family, I did not remember ever receiving love from anyone
apart of my performance. So, I worked hard and long, not in

rhythm with God's design, but to receive the love I craved. As a result, I worked nonstop in ministry. As president of Acts 29—a diverse, global family of about 800 church-planting churches—I worked eighty hours a week, seven days a week, 364 days a year. I took Christmas Day off, at least most of it. The more I produced, the more I felt I was worthy of a little bit of love.

God gave the Ten Commandments as a gift to his people. The fourth commandment reads, "Remember the Sabbath day, to keep it holy. . . . For in six days the LORD made heaven and earth, the sea, and all that is in them, and rested on the seventh day. Therefore, the LORD blessed the Sabbath day and made it holy" (Exodus 20:8, 11). A Sabbath is a day set aside holy unto the Lord. The late theologian R. C. Sproul explained this gift from God to humankind:

> Man was not made for restlessness. He was made for that inner peace and stability, and quietude that comes from the fulfillment of man's nature as it relates to God. There is a link between rest, that is, freedom from anxiety, freedom from this hard thing, loneliness, this awful empty feeling of anxiety that buffets us every day. There is a link between that rest, the Sabbath, and the purpose for which we were created, that is holiness. We were made in the image of God and we were made to have fellowship with God and we were made to reflect the character of God. In short, we were made for holiness.[2]

As leaders, we may desire to practice a consistent day of rest, but we may think we are too essential to what God will accomplish in our scope of responsibility. Paul Tripp believes this tendency leads to taking on more work than we can handle, which Tripp says he's experienced personally: "I begin to load the burden of the individual and collective growth of God's people onto my own shoulders."[3] Tripp is undoubtedly not the only one who has done this. Fear is a dominant emotion when we fail to Sabbath. We fear failure. We fear letting people down. We fear ourselves.

Bruce Waltke further explains the historicity of a Sabbath:

> By observing the Sabbath, Israel confesses regularly that their God is Lord of all. He made the Sabbath holy to celebrate his rest "from all the work of creating that he had done" (Gen. 2:3). [Meredith] Kline summarizes, "Observance of the Sabbath by man is thus a confession that Yahweh is Lord and Lord of all lords. Sabbath-keeping expresses man's commitment to the service of the Lord." In the creation, God ordains hierarchies of government in assigning the luminaries to govern day and night (1:18) and human beings to rule the earth (1:28). The Sabbath reminds God's image that they are his regents to serve him.[4]

I dishonored the Sabbath for decades. "[A Sabbath] will happen only as a result of a conscious choice," argues Dr. Matthew Sleeth.[5] Pete Scazzero described a Sabbath as a snow day.[6] I remember the snow days we had while growing up in Colorado. We would have no meetings, no responsibilities, and no deadlines, except for a spirited snowball fight in the park with the kids followed by snow angels and hot chocolate. And God gives us fifty-two snow days a year!

For those in local church ministry, your Sabbath is not going to be Sunday. Don't even try. But you need one day to allow God to have the room, space, and quiet needed to renew your soul. The three R's of a Sabbath are *resting*, *renewing*, and *reflecting* on God's grace and goodness. Spurgeon reminded his students that workers, artisans, and craftsmen would sharpen their tools, tune their instruments, and clean their brushes to be better at what they do. Those who use their brains and spirits must follow suit by not neglecting rest, renewal, and reflection. Spurgeon suggested that a walk in the woods, a ride in the countryside, or just breathing fresh air will sharpen the leader's tools.[7]

Rest Makes You Stronger

God is the Author and Creator of rest. He does not expect us to work nonstop. He designed one day every week to rest with his blessing.[8] Like the manna provided to the Israelites, God can provide seven days of sustenance in six days of work. A day of rest is a gift from a benevolent Father. Most of us today work too much, said Dr. Sleeth. He claimed that work is up 15 percent, and leisure is down 30 percent; and he predicted that things would only worsen.[9] Archibald Hart, professor of psychology at Fuller Theological Seminary, suggests that church leaders "need to build recovery time into their life after every period of stress. Failure to do so means the body never catches up; it never heals itself and gets back to its original state. It is extremely important to respect the Sabbath."[10]

An athlete must give their body time to heal after an intense workout. One workout resource explained how vital rest is to the body:

> It is rest that makes you stronger, because it is the rest that allows the muscles that you have broken down to heal and recover. It is the rest that allows you to recover so you can be strong, and thereby handle the increased weight, and increased number of sets and reps needed to gain further.[11]

Unless we rest, particularly after a stressful event, we will eventually be weaker and less productive and less beneficial to the Kingdom. I suspect that's contrary to your aim as a leader. As Spurgeon said, "a little pause prepares the mind for greater service in the good cause. . . . It is wisdom to take occasional furlough."[12]

Self-management is partnership with the Holy Spirit to control our emotions and act with transparency and integrity. To manage self means managing the whole person: body, spirit, and soul (mind, will, and emotions). Paul identifies this whole self in 1 Thessalonians 5:23: "Now may the God of peace himself sanctify you completely, and may your *whole spirit and soul and body* be kept blameless at the coming of our Lord Jesus Christ" (emphasis added). You matter to God—your whole self. Rest matters to God. It's his gift to us for his glory.

Leaders consistently fight four problem areas that are the results of poor self-management: time management, finances, loneliness, and vague boundaries. These can lead to burnout and depression. "Burnout is the final penalty for those who care too much as a part of their job," says Archibald Hart.[13] Spurgeon, who battled personal depression, explains, "Our work, when earnestly undertaken, lays us open to attacks in the direction of depression. Who can bear the weight of souls without sometimes sinking to the dust?"[14] Hart suggests that church leadership and ministry can be harmful to your health if you don't manage self:

> Burnout is a syndrome of emotional exhaustion, depersonalization, and reduced personal accomplishment among individuals who do people work of some kind. It is a response to the chronic, emotional strain of dealing extensively with people.[15]

Resting in Christ's Finished Work

The work of the gospel means that we no longer have to strive for achievement, approval, or acceptance. God has already accepted us through the person and work of Jesus Christ. One day, we will rest in his presence. This eternal rest is the ultimate joy, but not in our accomplishments. It is the day when we will cease from striving and receive eternal Sabbath rest. It will be the end of all uncertainty, conflict, anxiety, fatigue, financial shortage, and relational angst. Unfettered peace will dominate our final Sabbath. We find three general Sabbath constructs throughout Scripture.

First, when we consistently practice this rest from our labors, not as a binding duty but as a generous gift from God, we walk in line with the gospel. This rest isn't a day off in the typical sense. It is a day to realign with God. The writer of Hebrews confirms this: "So then, there remains a Sabbath rest for the people of God, for whoever has entered God's rest has also rested from his works as God did from his. Let us therefore strive to enter that rest, so that no one may fall by the same sort of disobedience" (Hebrews 4:9–11).

Our day of rest reflects the heart of God who "made heaven and earth, and on the seventh day . . . rested and was refreshed" (Exodus 31:17b). God didn't work one day and rest six or work three and half days and rest three and a half. He created us and knows what we need. Just as he designed us to work, he designed us to rest. Sabbath, therefore, is a gospel issue where we cease from striving for our salvation. Sabbath is a delight, not a duty (Isaiah 58:13–14).

Second, the Sabbath observance by the people of God was a shadow pointing to Christ's finished work (Colossians 2:16–17). Christ is the substance. The Sabbath was a shadow pointing to the real thing. Religious rigors will only heap more weight on our shoulders. Christ alone can carry your load. I'm not a Sabbatarian—that is, one who strictly observes a particular day as holy (Saturday or Sunday) forbidding any work. The old covenant observed the Sabbath as a shadow of the new covenant of rest in Christ. Paul forbids those who keep the Sabbath (Jewish believers) to condemn those who do not (Gentile believers) (Romans 14:5). Every day to the believer is a Sabbath because they rest from their spiritual labor for salvation (Hebrews 4:9–11). John Piper said, "the Sabbath is a gift of love to meet man's need, not an oppressive burden to make him [or her] miserable or proud."[16]

Third, our rest from work illustrates that our joy is not in our work, but in God, the One who gave us a purpose and plan for our life. Jobs come and go. Positions come and go—assignments from God change. Our allegiance is to a

Sovereign God who determines the allotted times and places for our ministry (Acts 17: 26). We work heartily for the Lord and not for people's approval (Colossians 3:23–24). Our work is for God's glory, and our rest is for God's glory. If not, our work and rest will be for our benefit and glory.

An American traveler planned a safari to Africa, and hired some local people to accompany him. On the first morning, they woke up early, traveled fast, and covered a great distance. The second morning was the same—woke up early, traveled quickly, and traveled far. The third morning, the same thing. But on the fourth morning, the local hired help refused to move. Instead, they sat by a tree in the shade well into the morning. The American traveler became irate and said to his translator, "This is a waste of valuable time. Can someone tell me what's going on here?" The translator looked at him, and calmly answered, "They're waiting for their souls to catch up with their bodies."[17]

How far back is your soul from catching up to your body?

Leaders' Restlessness Extends to Others

If we don't learn to rest in Christ, we will impose that unrest on others. It will affect all our relationships, beginning with God and extending to those closest to us. Our restlessness evokes a perception that others are never good enough or doing enough to satisfy us. We may view our relationship with God in the same way. We believe that we are never good enough, and thus we keep working harder to inch our way toward that elusive standard of acceptability.

The table below enumerates the differences between the rested leader and the restless leader.

Restless Leader	Rested Leader
My work is up to me.	I am dependent upon God, who gives me the ability and knowledge to accomplish work (Ex. 31:1–5).
My work is my identity.	I am a beloved child of God (Gal. 3:26).
If I don't work, I won't produce.	I am free to work heartily, as for the Lord (Col. 3:23; Eccl. 9:10).
I would prefer to burn out than rust out.	I am focused on glorifying God in my work (1 Cor. 10:31).
I am proud of my work and accomplishments.	I find joy in my sovereign Lord, who assigns me work for his glory (Acts 17:26).
I feel enslaved to my myriad of duties.	I am bound to Christ (Romans 7:1, 4–6).

Confessing Our Restlessness

The psalmist writes, "It is in vain that you rise up early and go late to rest, eating the bread of anxious toil; for he gives to his beloved sleep" (Psalm 127:2). We act without faith when we do not rest. We lack confidence in God's omnipotence and omnipresence. We do not exercise our faith to believe that there is a time to work and a time to rest, time for war, and a time for peace (Ecclesiastes 3:1–8). Here are four things we say when we fail to rest as leaders:

1. I don't trust God with my work, my ministry, my finances, or my family (Proverbs 3:5–6).
2. I don't respect how my Creator has designed me for both work and rest (Psalm 3:5; 4:8; 127:1–2).

3. I don't believe that my tired body will affect the state of my soul. I do not think that my soul craves rest (Psalm 62:1, 5).
4. I bow before the idols of performance, approval, comfort, and security.

Manage Self before Managing Others

John Calvin pointed out that if a leader does not pay careful attention to their life, that leader lacks the character to pay careful attention to the flock.[18] Part of self-management is managing rest as well as work. Here are five summary thoughts on resting:

1. God designed rest *for* humanity. God created the world, rested, and *blessed* the seventh day. As image-bearers of God, we can emulate this rest by completing our work, resting, and blessing others with a rested soul. Think about that. Our rested soul is a gift to those we lead. It is not selfish to rest. On the contrary, it is selfish to work so hard that our souls are famished when we serve others.
2. The earthly Sabbath reflects the eschatological reality of the eternal Sabbath rest to come. Practicing a Sabbath is expressing our rest in the finished work of Christ on our behalf. When we do, we focus on Jesus, the "founder, and perfecter of our faith" (Hebrews 12:2).
3. The Sabbath is a holy practice that gives glory to a sovereign, all-powerful God who is not bound to humankind's efforts. When we take time to rest, renew, and reflect, we affirm that there is a Creator and that we submit to his sovereign rule in every area of our life.

4. A leader may be in dire need of holy rest or holy recreation. Leaders need to reflect on their need for Christ. Taking time to acknowledge God as Lord of your life is a sign of trust. To deny that we don't need rest is to refuse the original created order that God established for the good and flourishing of creation. When leaders recognize their need to rest and take a sabbath, they do so in thankfulness to God.

5. Be watchful for our fellow church leaders. In this regard, we *are* their keeper. Be aware of our need for soul rest, manage it properly, and be mindful of other leaders around us. Help them pay attention to their need for rest as a means to holiness.

Rest in God's Grace, Love, and Acceptance

In the opening paragraph, I confessed my propensity to overwork. The Lord is redeeming that with greater self-management and awareness. I am still learning from my inclination to work for worthiness. I suspect it will be a lifelong effort. My workload is not diminishing at all, but I am allowing my soul to rest in Christ. I am humbling myself under the mighty hand of God. I am casting my anxieties on him. I know he cares for my burdens and I am managing my life in a holistic way. Satan is my enemy, and he will do everything possible to destroy me. I am resisting him and staying firm in the faith (1 Peter 5:6–9). Still, I am a serial repenter of restlessness.

Through the grace of God and the sacrifice of Jesus to impute to us his righteousness, we are beloved children of God in whom he is well pleased. We can't earn more favor from God. He doesn't demand more than the substitutionary atonement of his Son to declare us righteous. We don't have to act like a super leader. We are already God's adopted sons and daughters through the finished work of Christ. His grace, love, and acceptance—in spite of our actions—allows us to rest in him. "And what do you benefit if you gain the whole world but lose your own soul? Is anything worth more than your soul?" (Mark 8:36–37 NLT).

Spurgeon reminds us, "Rest time is not waste time. . . . We shall do more sometimes by doing less."[19] God gave you the God-glorifying gift of rest. Now, give the gift of a rested leader to those you lead.

Your Turn . . .

Prayer for a Rested Soul

Lord, from this day forward, I relinquish control. I will rest in you and your will to build your kingdom. I will enjoy every aspect of the journey on which you are taking me. I will worship you and glorify you by taking a Sabbath. I am declared righteous by the unmerited gift of Jesus. You love me despite my ongoing sins. Lead me to turn and see your glory—especially when the demands of ministry come like an avalanche. Help me to remember that you said, "Come to me, all who labor and are heavy laden, and I will give you rest. Take my yoke upon you, and learn from me, for I am gentle and lowly in heart, and you will find rest for your souls. For my yoke is easy, and my burden is light" (Matthew 11:28–30). Lord, help my unbelief.

Coaching Questions

1. What would it look like if you set aside a day of rest consistently every week?
2. Review the Restless/Rested Leader table (on page 90). Which side do you generally fall?
3. How will the gospel now inform your resting lifestyle?
4. How will you repent regarding any restlessness you might be experiencing?

Part Three
Relational Awareness

For the whole law is fulfilled in one word: "You shall love
your neighbor as yourself."

Galatians 5:14

Relational Awareness. I am thoughtful of others around me
and am compassionate about their needs (Matthew 9:35–38).
I listen to others as an act of love and can discern their unspoken actions, attitudes, and emotions (Philippians 1:9–10;
1 John 4:1). I seek to communicate with straightforwardness,
transparency, and honesty (Matthew 5:37).

8.
Love

Gospel-Shaped Leaders
Love the Church

The church . . . is a hospital in which nobody is completely well, and anyone can relapse at any time.

J. I. Packer, *A Quest for Godliness*

The church is the bride of Christ, but she isn't always a beautiful bride. The actions of church leaders toward congregants can make her difficult to love at times. As a staff pastor in various roles for over forty years, I am sad to say that the way I have seen church members treat one another weighs overwhelmingly on the unlovable side. I served at a church that demanded their staff members work seven days a week. A pastor docked me for time off to preach at my grandfather's funeral. One denominational leader told others I was a "wolf in the henhouse" simply because I held to a Reformed soteriology. One church demanded that my wife quit a job she loved because the "pastors' wives do not work." I have confronted lying from the pulpit, profanity in board meetings, and witnessed an elder pull out a handgun in a meeting. Yet, I love the local church—in spite of bad leadership—because she belongs to Christ. I have three books in my library: *The*

Subtle Power of Spiritual Abuse, *Recovering from Churches that Abuse*, and *Church Abuse of Clergy*.

These books exist as a testimony that the church urgently needs to change leadership practices. I was once a part of a church with a toxic culture. The pastor was brought up on charges and abruptly resigned. I left there to serve as a pastor in another church and I experienced a similar abusive environment where, again, the church fired the lead pastor.

I left those back-to-back experiences as a broken, skeptical, and disoriented man. I moved to Nashville and attended Immanuel Church, where my friend Ray Ortlund was the lead pastor. My wife and I sat in a two-person pew because we did not want to sit by anyone, talk to anyone, and certainly not hug anyone. Ray started the service with encouragement about an old Christian tradition of red-painted doors and declared that those who enter the church are safe from never measuring up and never belonging. He affirmed that inside the church, we experience God's love, and we belong to one another through the finished work of Christ. We questioned what Ray was saying because we had the opposite experience. "He is not lying, but he might be delusional," we wrongly thought. We came to believe he was prophesying the kind of church he hoped Immanuel would become. We stuck it out and, over time, realized it was exactly where we needed to find spiritual healing.

The church is not perfect, but she is the bride of Christ, and I love her. I picture Christ at the wedding altar awaiting his bride, the elect of God. God the Father escorts her down the aisle, but her dress is stained with mustard and ruffles are torn. Her hair is disheveled, lipstick smeared, and flowers wilted. As she limps down the aisle with one broken heel,

Jesus detects the smell of last night's alcohol and vomit. Yet, Christ passionately says, "There's my bride, and she is my beloved. I will receive her to make her holy. I will wash her with the water of the word. She will be my bride without spot or wrinkle" (see Song of Solomon 2:16; Ephesians 5:26–27). Augustine implored, "Let us honor her, for she is the bride of so great a Lord. . . . Great and unheard of is the bridegroom's gracious generosity; he found her a whore, he made her a virgin."[1] Christ, through his love, kindness, and mercy, joined himself to us, his cherished bride. We belong to Jesus and we belong to each other.

I love the church because Christ loves her in all her unloveliness. One day the bride of Christ will be pure and perfect and holy. For now, she needs healing. Jesus said, "Those who are well have no need of a physician, but those who are sick. I came not to call the righteous, but sinners" (Mark 2:17; cf. Matthew 9:12–13; Luke 5:31–32). The job of the church leader in some ways resembles a physician or nurse. It would be odd to hear an ER nurse asking in frustration, "Why are all these sick people here?" That's the job of medical personnel, and dealing with sick people is the job of the church leader. J. I. Packer remarked, "The church . . . is a hospital in which nobody is completely well, and anyone can relapse at any time."[2] Jesus said, "The Son of Man came not to be served but to serve, and to give his life as a ransom for many" (Mark 10:45). Gospel-shaped leaders come not to be served, pampered, worshiped, encouraged, and left alone. They are to shepherd with a Christlike sacrificial posture toward the endless needs of the flock.

Love the Church

A child or immature person demands that others meet their needs with immediacy. A child will often throw a tantrum, scream, or cry. An adult may become passive-aggressive, sulk, or lash out at others. A leader with spiritual maturity is relationally aware and is thoughtful of others around them and compassionate about their needs (Matthew 9:35–38). Relationally aware leaders listen to others as an act of love and can discern their unspoken actions, attitudes, and emotions (Philippians 1:9–10; 1 John 4:1). They can also apply biblical wisdom in relational circumstances (James 1:5). We can only love others when our attention is off self and directed toward others.

Christians are not exempt from being surly and stubborn, and these are the people God calls us to love. We will occasionally disagree with those in the church and it may lead to unnecessary conflicts. Francis Schaeffer offers five guidelines when disagreeing with others in the church:[3]

1. Approach these conflicts with deep tenderness toward the other person and tears of sorrow to confront a problem.
2. Demonstrate a seeable love for others (John 13:34), especially with major conflicts. When differences are great, so the love must be amplified.
3. Show love no matter the cost to self.
4. Approach the conflict to solve, not to win.
5. Remain united in Christ with fellow Christians in spite of differences. They are not disposable cups to discard. They are image-bearers of God.

Schaeffer essentially says disagreements among Christians cannot lead to divisions and we cannot be ambivalent if they do. We have to strive for reconciliation (Ephesians 4:26).

Jesus Is Worthy of Our Love

Jesus is the head of the church (Ephesians 1:22; 5:23; Colossians 1:18), and we are his body (Romans 12:4–5; 1 Corinthians 12:27). Paul proclaims, "And he is the head of the body, the church. He is the beginning, the firstborn from the dead, that in everything he might be preeminent" (Colossians 1:18). As such, he is preeminent; above all and worthy of our love. Jesus commands us to love God with our whole being (Matthew 22:37–38), and Jesus tells us to love him above family or anything else on this earth (Matthew 10:37). We love Jesus "because he first loved us" (1 John 4:19).

The church is the eternal bride of King Jesus, the Son of God who loved her and gave himself up so that she could be united with him and share in all that he is. Jesus is our Bridegroom and is worthy of our love.

Leonardo da Vinci invited a friend to offer critique of his masterpiece of the Last Supper. The friend remarked, "The most striking thing in the painting is the cup!" Da Vinci immediately took his brush and wiped out the cup and said, "Nothing in my painting shall attract more attention than the face of my Master!"[4] Nothing in our church ministry or our leadership shall attract more attention than the love we have for Jesus, including disagreements, misunderstandings, or theological differences.

Scripture explicitly states that Christ loved the church and demonstrated it through his crucifixion (Ephesians 5:25).

We are members of his body—a body that Jesus nourishes and cherishes (Ephesians 5:29–30). He sanctifies and cleanses his body to become holy and without blemish (Ephesians 5:26–27). The church is most unworthy and least lovable, but he loves her with his whole heart. Christ's love for the church is on display throughout Scripture. Human marriage is the reflection of the real love Christ has for the church. It is Christ's love that leads to the redemption of his bride through his blood (Ephesians 1:7).

Leaders Lead by Loving

Love flourishes in a church only when it is led by loving leaders. And, it's not some pedestrian love—it is Jesus's love. Jesus says, "A new commandment I give to you, that you love one another: *just as* I have loved you, you also are to love one another. By this all people will know that you are my disciples, if you have love for one another" (John 13:34–35, emphasis added). Christ commands us to love *just as* he loved us. We were his enemies, and he loved us (Romans 5:10). We were far from him, and he drew near us (Colossians 1:21–22). We were deep in sin, and he died for us (Romans 5:8). That means that in the church we love not only those who are lovely, but also those who are unlovely, annoying, accusatory, and critical. The world sees our love most evident when we love our enemies. The local church is a center stage for the amplification of Christ's love.

Leaders "consider how to stir up one another to love and good works" (Hebrews 10:24). We cannot lead a church only from our heads with a constant stream of sound doctrine. We must also lead from our hearts with endless love. Both head and heart must be present in our leadership. It is like going into an ice cream shop and asking for an ice cream cone. If the server gives you an empty cone, it is unsatisfying, like loveless doctrine. If you demand the ice cream and the server plops a scoop of mint chocolate chip in your hand, that is a messy situation and is akin to love without doctrine. But if the server gives you the ice cream in a cone, it is satisfying—love *and* doctrine, heart *and* head. A church needs both to exemplify Christ.

D. L. Moody preached seven sermons on the love of God from John 3:16. He studied what the Bible said about love and was amazed by his findings. He concluded that church work cannot be done without love. and his close associates said Moody "was never the same man." Moody said, "I look up the word 'Love,' and I do not know how many weeks I spent studying the passages in which it occurs, till at last, I could not help loving people. . . . There is no use trying to do church work without love. A doctor, a lawyer, may do good work without love, but God's work cannot be done without love.[5]

I've encountered leaders who loved the institution of the church and who loved theology but did not love God's people. God's work cannot be accomplished without love for Jesus and love for his bride.

Lead the Church as One Who Reflects Christ's Love for the Church

God ordained the visible church to be the manifestation of Christ to the world. God calls every Christian to reflect Christ to their neighbor. We show what Christ is like to those who are near and far from God. Gospel-shaped leaders reflect

Christ wherever they are—in the church, classroom, board-room, neighborhood, etc.

It is time to lead like Christ rather than by merging our sacred calling with profane practices. Too many church leadership teams have adopted "elemental spirits of the world" and "human precepts and teachings" that have "an appearance of wisdom" (Colossians 2:20–23). A pastor in Arizona told me how his elders held secret meetings and voted to remove him as the lead pastor. It was devastating and the church folded within three months. The church closed over the pride of her leaders. It showed the church body that their leaders had no clue how to obey Christ and lead in unity under Christ. Is this a compelling manifestation of Christ to the world? The London Baptist Confession (1689) explains what it means to lead like Christ:

> The members of these churches are saints by calling, visibly manifesting and evidencing (in and by their profession and walking) their obedience unto that call of Christ; and do *willingly consent to walk together,* according to the appointment of Christ; *giving up themselves to the Lord, and one to another, by the will of God, in professed subjection to the ordinances of the Gospel.*[6] (Emphasis added.)

You cannot effectively be a leader in the church without Christlike love for others. Leaders who lack spiritual maturity will seek to use their position as a secret doorway to receive love and power rather than a window to display Christ's love to others. Pastor-evangelist Robert Cleaver Chapman (1803–1902) was known as the apostle of love and was called "the saintliest man I know" by Charles Spurgeon.[7] Chapman said, "My business is to love others, not to seek that others love me."[8] Every church leader's business is to love others as Christ loved the church and gave himself for her. Jesus says, "For I have given you an example, that you also should do just as I have done to you" (John 13:15).

If we love Jesus, loving his bride is a decision we make in our minds that will grow, over time, in our hearts. She's worth it to Jesus and he lets us love her too.

Your Turn . . .

Prayer to Love the Church

Lord, cause me to love your bride as you do. Help me to receive her with devotedness, mercy, and kindness. I, your cherished bride, once strove after other lovers that could never satisfy. Cleanse me with the water of your Word. Make me holy and without blemish so that I can love my local church body as you love her.

Coaching Questions

1. How would you describe your love for the church?
2. What, in your church, tends to receive more attention than the love for Jesus?
3. What kind of leadership attitudes are necessary to display Christ's love for the body?
4. In what ways do you need to give up yourself to the Lord, and to one another to reflect Christ's love for the church?

9.
SERVE

Gospel-Shaped Leaders
Lead with Humility

[The really humble person] will not be thinking about
humility; he will not be thinking about himself at all.

C. S. Lewis, *Mere Christianity*

Like many young leaders, I struggled to learn the skill
of leading with humility. Things came quickly to me in
school, athletics, and business. Our stable family of five kids
was comfortable middle class. I had many good friends and
even an adult mentor. Being proud was something that my
parents promoted rather than tried to suppress. My natural
abilities fed the sin of my pride, and I dragged it into ministry. As a budding leader struggling with identity, especially
outside of athletics, I often positioned myself as the leader. I
believed I had earned the leadership position based on skill,
knowledge, experience, and sometimes by sheer resolve. I
wasn't blatant about it, and many people were unable to identify what was amiss. But they didn't say anything because I
was productive. If you are not self-aware, your success can
inhibit your emotional maturity, as it did mine. I led people
as if they needed to follow my direction or my teaching. I initially entered ministry with the passion for sharing the good

news of Jesus but soon became motivated by the success that it could garner me. But that is the opposite of how Jesus led.

Humility is a rare attribute among leaders. It really shouldn't be uncommon. The gospel calls us to humbly serve like Christ. Whereas pride is self-centered, humility is others-centered, and helping others is ostensibly the aim of leadership.

Leaders tend to vacillate between the extremes of arrogance and timidity. Arrogance is an expression of self-centeredness—seeking to receive undue attention and unmerited credit. Adulation can't be satisfied. Timidity is also self-centeredness—trying to avoid rejection or failure. This kind of pride can cloak itself in cowardice that appears humble. I was shy as a young boy, and I hated it. Now and then it creeps back up in the form of unassertiveness. Pride in either form is not an option for a leader.

Jesus said, "Apart from me you can do nothing" (John 15:5b). We are not able to do *some* things or *most* things or even *one* thing. Apart from Jesus, we can do *no* thing. We are not cooperatives, as some would believe, adding our part to God's grace. If we cut a branch off an apple tree, we would not expect the branch to continue producing apples. We cannot bear any fruit if we lead as if anything is dependent on our ability. God gifts the church with able leaders who disciple believers in Christ's fullness (Ephesians 4:11–13). The local church recognizes these gifts and provides authority to use them to advance the gospel (1 Timothy 4:14). Timid leaders fear being hurt instead of taking risks, and they selfishly do what is safe for them rather than what will produce good results for others. Timid leaders will not remain leaders for long and will likely experience mistreatment. Arrogant leaders will hurt others until they learn to lead with a humble spirit, or the organization removes them. The good news is that a lot of space exists between the two extremes of arrogance and timidity. This godly space is where the humble leader graciously resides and rests.

Utmost Evil—the Essence of Sin

C. S. Lewis explains that "the essential vice, the utmost evil, is pride. Unchastity, anger, greed, drunkenness, and all that are mere fleabites in comparison: it was through Pride that the devil became the devil: Pride leads to every other vice: it is the complete anti-God state of mind."[1] If pride is an anti-God posture, as Lewis purports, humility is pro-Jesus.

Gospel-shaped leaders must make a comfortable home for humility in their lives and give pride a daily eviction notice. According to John Stott, "Pride is our greatest enemy and humility our greatest friend."[2] Pride sneaks into our homes in the middle of the night and hides within the walls of our hearts. It seeps out in measured amounts to remain undetected until it finally consumes our entire being. Scripture implores us to "walk humbly with . . . God" (Micah 6:8b). Humility is not just a trait of good leadership, it is the essential foundation.

Clay Pots Are (Not) Amazing

We admire and applaud the awesome people in life. We appreciate musicians like Aretha Franklin, Eric Clapton, Mozart, Bach, and of course, Justin Bieber. Authors like Ernest Hemmingway, J. R. R. Tolkien, Agatha Christie, and C. S. Lewis captivate our imaginations. Scientists like Sir Isaac Newton, Louis Pasteur, Galileo, Jane Goodall, and Albert Einstein make our lives better. Great coaches inspire us: John Wooden, Don Shula, Vince Lombardi, Tony Dungy, and Paul "Bear" Bryant. Politicians like Margaret Thatcher, Abraham Lincoln, Winston Churchill, Nelson Mandela, Mahatma Gandhi, and have masterfully shaped our society. And then there are church leaders like Mother Teresa, Billy Graham, Charles Spurgeon, John Calvin, Martin Luther, Jonathan Edwards, and John Stott who propel us to aspire to know and serve God at a higher level. Where do you stand in this company of great people? You may feel inadequate, but you don't have to.

The gospel is contradictory to today's celebrity culture in the church. Gospel-shaped leaders do not revel in greatness; they strive to reveal the treasure. Paul says, "But we have this treasure in jars of clay, to show that the surpassing power belongs to God and not to us" (2 Corinthians 4:7). Does it seem strange to you that our weakness works in God's favor? We are born with a desire for victory. It is the plot of many good movies. In the movie *Taken*, the family experienced a good life until tragedy struck (kidnapping). Liam Neeson's character has a very particular set of skills, and he rescues his daughter and restores their comfortable living. The gospel storyline of goodness, tragedy, rescue, and restoration is familiar and appealing. But we distort the gospel when *we* want to be the hero. We are servants of the King. He alone is the hero, the protagonist in the good news storyline.

The extraordinary power of God resides in weak vessels. Jesus did not come like a lion, with power and strength; he came as a lamb, with meekness and humility. You don't have to be extraordinary. You are a clay pot that is ordinary, easily broken, and common. God's power is what is remarkable. Your success resides in your weaknesses, not in your strengths. The gospel alone informs this different way of leading. The clay pots hold the real treasure—the glorious light of the gospel (2 Corinthians 4). Gospel-shaped leaders are merely take-out containers. The goal of the take-out container is to hold something valuable, like the Szechuan chicken from Golden Dragon. The take-out container is incidental, disposable, and recyclable. We, too, are containers for the gospel—we are jars of clay, made from mud. God entrusts the gospel to us, and we must relinquish acting as if we're of equal value.

We're all clay pots for the King's most valuable treasure: the good news that sinners are made righteous by faith through the finished work of Christ. The more we try to be glorious on our own, the less the real treasure will be seen, admired, and valued. Leaders cannot be filled with Christ's power if they are filled with self. The focus must always be on the treasure and not on the vessel. When I bought my wife's costly diamond ring, the jeweler placed the ring on non-reflective black velvet so the diamond and setting would have no competition with light shining off the background. Had the jeweler placed the ring on a glittery mat, its sparkle would have been diminished.

The reason for the extreme contrast between the precious treasure and the soon-to-be-rubbish container is to show that the surpassing power belongs to God and not us. We distort the gospel's proclamation when we try to compete with the real treasure. We do not represent even a supporting role in the gospel story; we are the recipients of grace, and we are the boxes in which the gift arrives to others. Gospel-shaped leaders are not impressive, but the gospel is.

Break the Container

A broken, sobbing, unnamed woman shows up at the home of Simon the Pharisee where Jesus is dining (Luke 7:36–50).

She has been a notorious sinner in the community. It appears that she has an alabaster flask of expensive ointment to anoint Jesus for forgiving her sin. This flask isn't like the one your cousin gave you for being in his wedding. Alabaster is a stone that was used to carry perfume, ointment, and oil. It was often sealed to preserve the contents. Without fanfare, she pulls out the container, breaks it open, and pours it on Jesus's feet. It is perhaps her most valuable possession. She wipes his feet with her hair and tears and then shockingly kisses his feet. Do you remember others' reaction? Her expression of gratitude and love appalls everyone present except to Jesus.

The Pharisee despises her for her sinfulness and her audacity to wipe the ointment on Jesus's feet. But Jesus uses the event to explain the gospel to the Pharisee by telling him a story about two debtors who owed contrasting sums of money. He asks which of the two would be the most grateful, and the Pharisee rightly deduces that it would be the one who owes the most money. Jesus forgives the sinful woman and releases her in peace. The broken treasure lavishly releases the healing ointment.

We either become the broken flasks, or we can pigheadedly remain intact. The costly ointment is the gospel. When the clay breaks and the contents pour out, it renews and fills the room with the aroma of healing and forgiveness to sinners like this woman who did nothing to deserve Jesus's mercy. A gospel-shaped leader doesn't demand to be the pretentious vase in the foyer of the house, but rather the humble clay pot that carries the treasure and that is broken to release the light of the glory of God through Christ. The pleasant aroma of the woman's ointment fills the room in contrast to the stench of the Pharisee's self-righteousness. The balm of forgiveness can heal, whereas self-righteousness only decays everything around it.

Pushing the 'Bw'ow

When my grandson was eighteen months old, I put him in a wheelbarrow and wheeled him around the backyard while he squealed with delight. When I got tired, which didn't take long, I convinced him to get out of the wheelbarrow. But he wasn't done with the one-wheeled vehicle that made him so happy. He didn't want to ride this time; he wanted to push it as I did. Since he wasn't tall enough to reach the handles, he grabbed the carriage portion between the handles and pushed with all his might, but it didn't budge. I grabbed the handles from behind him, which took the weight off and gently pushed it forward in the proper way while he continued to shove on the carriage walking along. He thought he was cool to move that big yellow wheelbarrow all on his own. While he continued pushing, he looked back at me to make sure I saw how strong he was. "Way to go, buddy," I encouraged him. He pushed even harder, believing he was moving what he called the 'bw'ow. I could have said, "Buddy, you are a weak, insignificant little runt who cannot even pronounce wheelbarrow, so stop trying to push." I love my grandson, so we kept pushing it together. He took all the credit, and I received all the joy.

That's our role as church leaders. We aren't the ones pushing anything—God is. But we deceive ourselves if we believe our abilities are indispensable.

We Are Dead to Self

Refuse to take credit for what the Lord is accomplishing through your leadership or ministry. In the ninth century BC, Adad-Nirari II was King of Assyria. Assyria oppressed the world with its dominating evil power, and its kings were dictatorial tyrants. King Adad-Nirari II said, "I am royal, I am lordly, I am mighty, I am honored, I am exalted, I am glorified, I am powerful, I am all-powerful, I am brilliant, I am lion-brave, I am manly, I am supreme, I am noble."[3] I am sad to say, that sounds like a lot of Christian conference talks. It is said of Jesus, "He made himself nothing" (Philippians 2:7a NIV). Think of that. The King of kings, Lord of lords, co-creator of the vast universe made himself nothing.

Simon Sinek's book *Leaders Eat Last* is based on the US Marines' unwritten practice. Sinek noted that the lowest-ranked soldiers always eat first, and the most senior officers eat last. One officer explained to Sinek that Marine officers view leadership as a responsibility, not as a rank. The officer said, "It's not about being in charge; it's about *taking care of those in your charge.*" That's what leadership is, and that illustrates what a gospel-shaped leader does as well. Jesus emptied himself and took on the form of a servant and humbled himself, fulfilling his calling from the Father to die in our place (Philippians 2:7–8).

Jesus says, "Come to me, all who labor and are heavy laden, and I will give you rest. Take my yoke upon you, and learn from me, *for I am gentle and lowly in heart,* and you will find rest for your souls. For my yoke is easy, and my burden is light" (Matthew 11:28–30, emphasis added). Jesus can make this offer for all those who are weary, tired, disappointed, fed up, depressed, hurting, beat up, filled with regrets, anxious, fearful, sexually confused, and exhausted. Jesus, the lowly humble servant, receives all who come to him.

Jesus was free of self-importance, free from focusing on his interests. Our life, posture, and attitude can flow from this burden-lifting, grace-giving, rest-producing, life-enriching source: the gentle and humble Savior. A self-important position is not God-given; it is stolen because there is no position for leaders who are more interested in themselves than those they are leading.

The best way of dying to self is by serving others. It is a decision we must make every day. We can also die to self by always exalting the King's accomplishments and not ours. Dying to self is an expression of the gospel. Jesus shows us how:

> Have this mind among yourselves, which is yours in Christ Jesus, who, though he was in the form of God, did not count equality with God a thing to be grasped, *but emptied himself,* by taking the form of a servant, being born in the likeness of men. And being found in human form, *he humbled himself* by *becoming obedient to the point of death, even death on a cross.* (Philippians 2:5–8, emphasis added)

As I wrote in the opening paragraph of this chapter, I struggled with pride in my younger years because I thought it was a positive attribute. I related to the brash, quick-to-act, aggressive Peter. He was my favorite apostle. He stepped out of the boat onto the water when everyone sat still. He cut off the ear of the high priest's servant in the garden of Gethsemane. He spoke up when others were silent. I thought *that* was leadership. God allowed me to experience humiliating trials, and it has made me a better person and leader. God transformed Peter as well, and Peter testified to this in his first epistle: "Likewise, you who are younger, be subject to the elders. Clothe yourselves, all of you, with humility toward one another, for 'God opposes the proud but gives grace to the humble'" (1 Peter 5:5). Peter learned the hard way and so did I. We can humbly submit to the shaping hand of Christ and be useful leaders in others' lives. Follow Jesus; he will show us how.

Your Turn . . .

Prayer for Humility

Lord, apart from you, I can do nothing. I know this and yet, pride creeps in like a slithering snake trying to convince me to take credit for what you are doing through my feeble efforts. Enable me to walk humbly before you. I am an ointment flask for your glory. You are the healing oil. Make me gentle and lowly in heart and empty of self. I revel that I can be your servant.

Coaching Questions

1. What is one instance of your leading with pride? How could you have led with humility instead?
2. How does a desire for fame or attention misrepresent the gospel?
3. What needs to be broken in your life to display humility?
4. What ministry accomplishments do you tend to attribute to *your* abilities?
5. How has your recognition, fame, or success taken away from the incomparable beauty of the person and work of Jesus?

10.
SPEAK

Gospel-Shaped Leaders Communicate with Grace-Filled Candor

> A lamblike, dovelike spirit and temper is the true and
> distinguishing disposition of the hearts of Christians.
>
> Jonathan Edwards

I served closely with Jim at a large multisite church that was led by a domineering lead pastor. Jim was a uniquely gifted pastor with a compelling personality, intimidating drive, a creative mind, and a passion for reaching young adults who hadn't considered church. He convinced college graduates to raise funds and come work at the campus he led. The church grew to three services that consisted mostly of college students, recent college graduates, and empty nesters (like me) who loved to serve within this dynamic church. He made a massive impact on that liberal college town. But Jim suddenly resigned from the church and moved twenty-five hundred miles away. He couldn't shake the emotional exhaustion of the abusive and domineering lead pastor. He wasn't the only one who was on the receiving end of this oppression. He knew the extent of the lead pastor's brutal behavior, but this young, exceptional leader was still physically shaking even a year later while recalling what happened to him. This promising young leader is no longer in ministry.

The way a leader speaks to others either inspires or suffocates spiritual discipleship. Any immature leader can be forceful, unheeding, and unloving. Only a true man or woman of God can be gentle.[1] Paul tells the Galatian leaders, "If anyone is caught in any transgression, *you who are spiritual should restore him in a spirit of gentleness.* Keep watch on yourself, lest you too be tempted. Bear one another's burdens, and so fulfill the law of Christ" (Galatians 6:1–2, emphasis added). The biblical idea of restoring a person means to mend or repair or put a bone back into place. You certainly do not want an orthopedic doctor using brute force to set your broken bone. A gospel-shaped leader exercises a spirit of gentleness in ministry, especially in broken circumstances. As James Dean (creator of "Pete the Cat") said, "I am trying to find the courage to be tender in my life. I know violence is weakness. Only the gentle are ever really strong." Jesus was both gentle and strong (Matthew 11:28). We cannot avoid conflict and misunderstanding, so we must adequately address it with what I call grace-filled candor.

Leaders set the tone for demonstrating the fruit of the Spirit. "But the fruit of the Spirit is love, joy, peace, patience, kindness, goodness, faithfulness, gentleness, self-control; against such things, there is no law" (Galatians 5:22–23). A gospel-shaped leader is one who is spiritual *and* gentle. Spiritual leaders "admonish the idle, encourage the fainthearted, help the weak, be patient with them all" (1 Thessalonians 5:14). But a leader must also be gentle in dealing with people—even difficult people. Gentleness is a distinctive characteristic of those who walk by the Spirit.

When our two sons were young, my wife and I determined never to raise our voices to seek control over their behaviors. God gave us the responsibility to raise them to respect us and God. They didn't always agree with our directives, but we were gentle with them while remaining firm in our beliefs. Sometimes people need just enough gentleness to see past their stubbornness. Yelling and demanding doesn't work in the long run. One afternoon, one of my sons stubbornly refused to complete his homework regardless of how much his mother tried to convince him. She debriefed me when I came home. I told him he didn't have to do his homework. You should have seen Jeannie's face as she stood to the side listening! He said, in disbelief, "I don't?" I said, "No, but if you don't do your homework, you can't go to your basketball game tonight." His homework was done in ten minutes and he brought it to me fully dressed in his basketball uniform. Fast-forward thirty years and I watch with joy as my son treats his kids in the same grace-filled way.

Four Ways to Speak to Others

Confronting others is exhausting. But it is even more tiring to avoid conflict. Relational strain will grow like weeds in an untended field. The best way to lead is by addressing problems in a spirit of gentleness and with grace-filled candor. Apply the attitude of a mother to a nursing child. "But we were gentle among you, like a nursing mother taking care of her own children" (1 Thessalonians 2:7). Paul Tripp advocates for a gentle approach as well: "Gentle talk does not come from a person who is angry and looking to settle the score. It comes from the person who is speaking not because of what he wants from you but what he wants for you."[2]

On the table, "Four Ways to Speak to Others," the vertical axis measures the level of relational connectivity with the person(s) you are leading. The horizontal axis measures the intentionality in your interactions. The vertical axis goes from intimacy at the top to indifference at the bottom. The horizontal axis goes from passivity on the left to intentionality on the right.

If you are leading a specific project or team, intentionality is high while intimacy can be low. If you are attending a company social event, intentionality usually is low but intimacy is higher. Let's explore the four ways to speak to others: compliance, critique, control, and grace-filled candor.

Four Ways to Speak to Others

Intimacy

Compliance
- Passive, friendly interactions
- Normal in casual settings
- Unhelpful in leadership

Candor
- Intentional ministry environment & close relationships
- Honest, grace-filled communication

Passive ← | 1 | 4 | → **Intentional**
| 2 | 3 |

Critique
- Passive goals and little relationship
- Hurtful talk, judgmental
- Unaware of others' situation

Control
- Intentional ministry goals without closeness to others
- Demand of others for success
- Fear of failure

Indifference

Compliance, in the top left quadrant, is the mark of an intimate albeit passive interaction. It is the type of interaction that is normal and natural when exchanging pleasantries in social situations among church members, co-workers, and neighbors. In leadership contexts it has limited usefulness. In this quadrant, we experience an elevated level of relational connectivity without candid conversations about another person's actions, attitudes, character, or competence. As a result, external sources of conflict are glossed over without directly dealing with the root causes or the relational dysfunctions. This can be unhelpful for the leader.

If we aren't able to move beyond compliance in our relationships, we may have made an idol of approval. Leaders whose interactions lie in this quadrant are most likely motivated by a desire to avoid loneliness or perception of non-inclusivity. They often fear rejection and, therefore, rarely confront or point out inadequacies in others. This leader values the other person and sacrifices honesty to maintain a relationship or at least an appearance of one. They do not risk that relationship by pushing for more productive outcomes. It is foolish for a leader only to have agreeable friends. It is sad that some marriages operate in this quadrant.

Critique, in the bottom left quadrant, characterizes the interactions of the person who interacts with another without pursuing or possessing a personal relationship (they are indifferent) and without real intentionality (they are passive). This is the congregant who criticizes the sermon but rarely prays for the pastor. Critical thinking is necessary for an effective leader as they look for better ways and strategies to accomplish a goal. However, a leader also needs to seek the best interests of those they are leading. Critique is when leaders *walk over* people instead of *walking alongside* them. Constructive criticism is only helpful if it involves a personal relationship and an agreed-upon goal of both parties. Followers who remain in this quadrant may get frustrated, angry, or discouraged. Leaders who operate in this quadrant will drive people away.

The corrective is to get to know the other person at a deeper level. If we do not have a personal relationship with someone, we will never really be able to lead them. Once we know another person and are praying with them and for them, it is difficult to criticize their actions and words. Insecure leaders tend to critique others. They fear being intimate and vulnerable. The Pharisees—the self-righteous leaders in Jesus's time on earth—embody this critique mode.

Control, in the bottom right quadrant, characterizes the interactions of the leader who speaks to others to demand they get things done. They fail to focus on a meaningful relationship with those they are leading. My family makes fun of me when I try to order from an outside menu at a drive-through. I like to look at people, smile, and politely ask them to fulfill my order. I rarely attempt drive-through ordering because I don't hear them or they don't hear me. I tried it once when I was alone, and I still failed despite the absence of their impending and sure mocking of my failure in this basic skill. I couldn't get my order across. I don't like to yell directives at people. I parked and walked in and the workers were talking about me! I left them a big tip. Some leaders are drive-through leaders who yell commands at others and demand they get it just right. It never works for long. This type of leader gets angry and lashes out with harsh words or physical actions and then walks away from the wreckage they create. They commonly belittle others and attack them when they are most vulnerable.

People are willing to get things done if there is a set goal or intentionality is high. But they will not continue being led by an aloof leader or one who has made an idol of power and control. This type of leader is motivated by success and fears failure. Therefore, they push, manipulate, threaten, and sometimes attempt to motivate others with prestige, position, or payroll. These leaders are more interested in their success than in the development of others.

The corrective is to lead with humility and teamwork, rather than by threats and demands. To develop leadership skills in others, this leader needs to draw people out by asking questions about the best course of action.

The passive-aggressive person lives in the critique and control quadrants. Merriam-Webster defines "passive-aggressive" as displaying behavior characterized by negative feelings, resentment, and aggression in an unassertive passive way. Passive-aggression is an emotionally abusive behavior because the leader does not directly deal with the person's problem, inadequacy, or failure. This type of leader, instead of communicating honestly when disappointed, may allow their feelings to fester over time. They shut off emotionally healthy responses, and wrongly try to keep the upper hand by always making others wonder what they are thinking.

Candor, in the top right quadrant, characterizes the grace-filled interactions of the wise leader. It is the ideal quadrant from which to communicate to those you lead. Candor is truthful frankness directly addressed with another person. A grace-filled posture occurs when you extend kindness and love, even if a person's actions do not justify it. A gospel-shaped leader speaks kindly to others in a safe environment and explains how their actions adversely affect others.

The goal of grace-filled candor is to find a solution to the conflict while deepening relationships with others. I am sad to say that this kind of candor is not typical, and that is precisely why gospel-shaped leaders stand out from other leaders. Being grace-filled isn't waving a white flag and surrendering. It is speaking forthrightly about the problem *without* attacking the other person and then, if possible, collaborating with that person for a resolution. Of course, those we are leading do not always respond positively, and we may have to persevere with grace.

Grace-filled candor requires having an intimate relationship with the other person. Leaders must not avoid this vulnerable space. They are intentional in their focus and objectives, yet lead others with a shepherd's staff rather than an electric cattle prod. Loving leaders can speak with candor because those they are leading are aware of this love for their best interests. Jesus describes himself as the Good Shepherd and beckons others to follow him (John 10). The apostle Paul implies that grace-filled candor (speaking the truth in love) results in a healthy, mutually benefiting organization:

> Instead, we will *speak the truth in love, growing in every way more and more like Christ,* who is the head of his body, the church. He makes the whole body fit together perfectly. As each part does its own special work, it helps the other parts grow, so that the whole body is healthy and growing *and full of love.* (Ephesians 4:15–16 NLT, emphasis added)

Leadership Is Always Relational

Leadership is all about relationships. Bonhoeffer writes, "The Christian needs another Christian who speaks God's Word to him. He needs him again and again when he becomes uncertain and discouraged, for by himself he cannot help himself without belying [contradicting] the truth."[3] Bonhoeffer expresses what we know, but sometimes fail to apply: we need each other to consistently display the gospel in our lives. Gospel-shaped leadership requires relational awareness—the thoughtful, compassionate shepherding of others around you. If we are not exercising conflict-resolution skills, our life will be needlessly difficult. For the leader, conflict is not always wrong, even if we are the recipient; it may allow us to clarify expectations, establish principles, and build relationships. If we are the ones who caused the conflict, it will enable us to apologize and make amends if damage occurred. We learn by our mistakes, and we grow by our mishaps. Gospel-shaped leaders learn to transform struggles into solutions.

Gospel-shaped leaders don't react in kind to negative behaviors, attitudes, and words; they find suitable answers. They try to understand others' perspectives before speaking. If appropriate, they empathetically ask the offended person about the cause of their emotional state. Often the other person is not even aware of their emotions. Their actions may result from something entirely outside of their relationship with anyone caught in their crossfire. Offensive people often lash out at those nearby rather than direct energy toward the cause. Sometimes people do not know why they are frustrated or angry and don't need a lecture; they need a mature emotional response.

Gospel-shaped leaders limit addressing conflict with people outside their relationship circle. The internet and social media warp this concept. We can only lead those with whom we are in a relationship. We don't have to address every injurious action or rude comment expressed. If we are not in a relationship with or responsible for the person doing the damage, we can let it go or show kindness.

An older member of a church where I was lead pastor said in a church meeting, "I see that we have moved the communion table out of the sanctuary. I guess the pulpit is next." This widow had been saying things like this for years, long before I became pastor. No one ever confronted her, so she continued with caustic words. Her fellow church members often excused her comments by saying, "Oh, that's just Maggie." I was trying to change the church culture, so I said, "I am sorry that you feel like some of the changes we are making are not right. But your comments are not helpful. They are misinformed and hurtful. I lent the communion table to a new church that held their very first communion service this morning. It will be back next Sunday." She and everyone remained silent. No one had ever challenged Maggie. She was feared by young and old because she knew how to manipulate a church meeting with barbed attacks on the leadership. It required grace-filled candor to diffuse her fear of change. She didn't need a reactive tirade, although that was my first inclination. She needed to be shown grace as a mature emotional response. Maggie and I became good friends from that point forward. I asked her to help me solve some problems, and she was helpful and generous.

Apply Grace-Filled Candor as a Generous Encourager

Grace-filled candor is built by regularly encouraging others around us. Encouragement deepens relationships and opens the door to honest communication. It baffles me that an encouraging leader is a rarity. Leaders certainly have a lot of responsibilities to manage in their work, families, and personal lives. But the people they lead need more encouragement than directives or critique.

Gospel-shaped leaders are generous encouragers—not stingy with words of affirmation, compassion, praise, and honor. Let's commit to build up men and women under our care and embolden them with godly courage. If we see a person in need and fail to meet their need, John's epistle warns us, we are withholding the love of God (1 John 3:17). Often, people do not need food and clothing but are *starving* for a word of encouragement. Gospel-shaped leaders understand the power of words. "Do not withhold good from those to whom it is due, when it is in your power to do it" (Proverbs 3:27). A leader's words of encouragement have immense benefits. Roy Bennett, the Zimbabwean politician, says, "One word of encouragement can be enough to spark someone's motivation to continue with a difficult challenge."[4] We will never know how influential our words can be until we practice encouragement regularly.

Grace-Filled Candor Keeps Pursuing Others

The world cannot build a community with dissimilar people. Only Jesus can unite people of various cultures, backgrounds, and ethnicities and make us one. One of the core values of a church I started was "relentless love." Without Jesus, we will stop pursuing others. Without Jesus, we will quickly discard each other.

God instructs Jonah to warn Nineveh of its wickedness and to tell them to repent. Jonah disobeys God's command, and boards a boat headed in the opposite direction. Our response would be to wave goodbye to this disloyal and selfish leader. We would move on, but God does not. His love is relentless. God sends a violent storm to disrupt Jonah's travel plans. When the panicked sailors find out that Jonah is the cause of the storm, they throw him overboard. But that isn't the end of Jonah because God still pursues him. He orders an oversized oceanic Uber (a great fish) to swallow him and give him a three-day and three-night ride to convince him to return to God. From the fish's belly, among the partially digested fish and gastric juices, Jonah finally cries out to God for help (Jonah 2:1–9). God tells the seafaring taxi to drop Jonah off on dry land in order to give him a second chance to warn Nineveh.

We would have chosen a replacement for Jonah, but grace-filled candor relentlessly pursues. Jonah preaches to Nineveh, and the entire country, including the king, turns to God. That was a successful campaign by all standards. However, their repentance ticks Jonah off. The Bible says he was exceedingly angry at the mercy of God toward Nineveh. I would have given up on Jonah when he rejects God's call. I would no doubt have given up on him as he sulks. Jonah did what God tells him, and God saves over 120,000 people from death. As a result, Jonah fumes like a teenager without a good Wi-Fi signal. That kind of attitude can destroy the morale of any office party. It's better if they weren't there, we believe, than infect the rest of the team. But God keeps pursuing Jonah despite his surly and immature behavior.

God shows even more kindness to Jonah by causing a shade plant to grow over Jonah's head while he sits and sulks. God's kindness is unfathomable. We would reason that this would encourage Jonah's negative behavior. But God wants to teach Jonah a lesson, and so the plant is soon destroyed first by a worm and then by the hot sun and wind. This makes Jonah angry again, but God responds again with grace by pointing out that if Jonah can feel sorry about a plant why shouldn't God care about the many thousands of people in Nineveh. God was not quick to discard Jonah while he was expressing emotional immaturity. We need to rethink writing off rude people.

Jonah knew God's character as "merciful, slow to anger and abounding in steadfast love" (Jonah 4:2). Jonah needed the Lord's grace-filled candor to work on his heart. Leaders can display the gospel by practicing lingering love for sulking saints.

Grace-Filled Candor Displays the Gospel

When we speak with gentle honesty to others, it is a beautiful picture of God's nature. God shows his love toward us by sending Jesus to die for us while we are sinning (Romans 5:8). God reconciles us, through the death of Jesus, *while we were enemies* of his (Romans 5:10). In fact, on the cross, as people were mocking him, Jesus prays, "Father, forgive them, for they know not what they do" (Luke 23:34). It is grace that pursues us, grace that saves us, and grace that sustains us. It is not uncommon to demonstrate grace to those who deserve it, but only the gospel shows kindness to those who are far from earning it.

Grace-filled candor doesn't shortchange the truth. It only works when honesty is a non-negotiable characteristic. It boldly and confidently presents the truth of the gospel with grace.

Gospel-shaped leaders speak the hard truth to others in four ways:

1. **We tell the hard truth only to those with whom we have a relationship.** We don't have the right to tell every Walmart shopper to get out of their pajamas and

put on clothes before shopping—unless it's our aunt.

2. **Our speech is always gracious (Colossians 4:6).** The goal of grace-filled candor is to help others. The opposite is to accuse harshly or twist the truth for our benefit.

3. **We do it verbally and never in written form.** The best way to apply grace-filled candor is face-to-face. An alternative is some other auditory communication so that the love in our voice can be clearly heard.

4. **Our grace-filled candor is always clear, correct, caring, and Christlike.** We must be clear about what we are addressing; make sure it's accurate; express care for the person; and represent a gentle, shepherding Redeemer.

Jonathan Edwards reminds us, "A lamblike, dovelike spirit and temper is the true, and distinguishing disposition of the hearts [and words] of Christians."[5] Grace-filled candor is necessary for leadership in the church and home. You can be strong and gentle in your demeanor. Jesus showed us how.

Jim, from the opening paragraph, would surely have had a different outcome if that leader had exercised gentle speech. Our words will shape the lives of others. Like Jesus, the gentle Shepherd, always apply grace-filled candor—especially to the people we lead.

Your Turn . . .

Prayer

Lord, I want to demonstrate the fruit of the Spirit in my words: love, joy, peace, patience, kindness, goodness, faithfulness, gentleness, and self-control. Enable me to speak the truth in love, growing in every way to be more and more like

Christ. Let my words always be gracious and useful for the kingdom.

Coaching Questions

1. In your experiences, what was the outcome of someone leading without gentleness?
2. Review the table. Consider the four ways to speak to others. In what quadrant do you naturally lead, and why?
3. What would it require for you to become an encouraging leader?
4. What principles from this chapter do you need to put into practice?

Part Four

Relational Management

I therefore, a prisoner for the Lord, urge you to walk in
a manner worthy of the calling to which you have been
called, with all humility and gentleness, with patience,
bearing with one another in love, eager to maintain the
unity of the Spirit in the bond of peace.

Ephesians 4:1–3

Relational Management. I can apply biblical wisdom in relational circumstances (James 1:5). I commit to develop other
people to build up the organization (Ephesians 4:11, 16). I
seek to resolve relational conflicts (Philippians 4:2). I seek to
reconcile my broken relationships (Matthew 5:23–24; 18:15;
Romans 12:18). I can build relationships to accomplish goals
(Hebrews 10:24–25).

11.
GUIDE

Gospel-Shaped Leaders
Relate as Family

> Our relationship with each other is the criterion the world
> uses to judge whether our message is truthful—Christian
> community is the final apologetic.
>
> Francis Schaeffer, *The Mark of the Christian*

With tears in her eyes, a young woman told me about how her church (and employer for over ten years) abruptly fired her from a job she loved. A few months prior, the church board fired the lead pastor for domineering and misusing his power, among other things. His departure negatively affected the church's financial contributions, of course. So, the leaders said they needed to right-size their church staff, and they called her into a meeting that lasted no more than five minutes. Effective immediately, they released her from employment, took away her church keys and computer, and then sent her home. She wasn't allowed to say goodbye to her fellow staff or to transfer her responsibilities to others. Within two hours, they also shut down her email. She was not let go for incompetence or a violation of church policy. Her firing was no fault of her own, yet they treated her in a profane manner.

The unfortunate irony is that the same church who fired their pastor for misuse of power fired this employee in a similarly barbaric fashion. She described this experience as inhumane, and it eerily reminded her of the feelings she experienced as a child when her father verbally abused her. She now has a cynical view of every male church leader. I don't blame her. Paul tells Timothy, "Do not rebuke an older man but encourage him as you would a father, younger men as brothers, older women as mothers, younger women as sisters, in all purity" (1 Timothy 5:1–2). We demonstrate the gospel when we treat members of the church as fathers, brothers, or daughters, sisters, or mothers. Respecting them as family honors God, and it makes a world of difference—for the person, for the church, and the church leader.

I think the church has adopted the business world's best practices for how she functions. I believe this is a fundamental mistake with dire consequences. Church leadership does not consist of business leadership principles spiritualized with a sprinkling of Bible verses, but rather, Christ-centered family leadership. It's a major difference. Now, understand, I implement sound business principles in my home, like a budget, a calendar, goal-setting, investing, and so forth. I am not opposed to business principles, per se. However, in a family, those principles are emphasized and prioritized differently than in a business. As we lead our home, so we lead the church. Church leaders must demonstrate competent leadership in the home to be qualified for church leadership because it is the same attitude and approach. A church overseer "must manage his own household well, with all dignity keeping his children submissive, for if someone does not know how to manage his own household, how will he care for God's church? . . . Let deacons each be the husband of one wife, managing their children and their own households well (1 Timothy 3:4–5, 12).

Gospel-shaped leaders relate as familial leaders. Churches are prone to choose their leaders based on how well they manage their businesses. Business savvy is not the criterion for church leadership. The person who is unable to govern their home is unfit to govern the church. People may be able to lead a company of paid employees, and even draw respect from the community, but unable to influence their family to grow in holiness and faith in Christ (cf. Titus 1:6). If we struggle in our leadership in the home, we will struggle in the church.

Guide God's Family with Emotional Maturity

Relational management is crucial in the church. Paul gives us the template for Christian leadership: "I therefore, a prisoner for the Lord, urge you to walk in a manner worthy of the calling to which you have been called, with all *humility* and *gentleness*, with *patience*, bearing with one another in *love*, eager to maintain the *unity* of the Spirit in the bond of *peace*" (Ephesians 4:1–3, emphasis added). Paul urges every church business meeting, staff meeting, counseling session, financial review, and so forth to be marked with humility, gentleness, patience, love, unity, and peace.

We must learn to lead by equipping others to lead, which is God's plan for the church (Ephesians 4:11–16). It is the difference between driving a car and teaching another to drive with the same level of skill and intuition. Leaders often ask *what* is needed, but they also must ask *who* this will develop. It was intuitive to me as a father to take every opportunity to build character into my children. It took me a lot longer to realize this in the ministry because I lacked examples in my church experience.

Developing others requires an intentional expenditure of energy by the leader toward the disciple. That interaction can cause unintentional conflicts, and leaders must promptly manage that relationship by humility, gentleness, patience, love, unity, and peacemaking rather than by force.

The family dynamic is the best teacher for managing relationships. Parents demonstrate to their children how to manage stress, conflict, loss, mistakes, and misunderstandings. Christian leaders act as mothers and fathers and older siblings of a family. When leaders learn to treat others with the mindset of a spiritual mother or father, they will know how to approach others in the church. It changes the tone and the outcome considerably.

God Adopts Us into His Family

The adoption of God's people into his family is one of the most profound realities in Christianity. We are not slaves or servants or employees of God's; we are his children. J. I. Packer considers adoption to be "the highest privilege of the gospel: higher even than justification." He added, "Adoption is a *family* idea, conceived in terms of *love*, and viewing God as *father*." God takes us into his family and makes us his children and heirs. Packer concludes, "To be right with God the Judge is a great thing, but to be loved and cared for by God the Father is greater."[1] Paul explains it succinctly to the believers in Galatia:

> But when the fullness of time had come, God sent forth his Son, born of woman, born under the law,

to redeem those who were under the law, *so that we might receive adoption as sons.* And *because you are sons,* God has sent the Spirit of his Son into our hearts, crying, "Abba! Father!" So *you are no longer a slave, but a son,* and if a son, then an heir through God. (Galatians 4:4–7, emphasis added)

God declares us to be his sons and daughters. That fact opens the door to intimacy and communion with our Father. A son is not a slave, but a welcomed member of the family. In the parable of the prodigal son, the older brother says to his father, "Look! All these years I've been *slaving* for you" (Luke 15:29 NIV). Contrast this with John's words, "See what kind of love the Father has given to us, that we should be called *children* of God; and so we are" (1 John 3:1).

John Wesley tirelessly worked to not only serve the church, but also inmates, orphans, and the poor in eighteenth century England. Although he did many good works, he was not a convert of Christ until later. Looking back on that time, Wesley reflected, "I had even then the faith of a *servant*, though not that of a *son*."[2]

Salvation means an orphan child becomes an adopted child that a family loves and welcomes as its own (John 14:18; Romans 8:15). Adoption is only possible through Jesus Christ. Since every believer is a brother or sister in Christ, it will change how a leader interacts with other believers, especially those within the same church.

If we view God through the lens of a slave, we will demand that same overbearing allegiance from others. On the other hand, if we enjoy the biblical image as an adopted child of God, we will see others as brothers and sisters, mothers and fathers, sons, and daughters. Sometimes that means we will have to exercise discipline as a demonstration of our love. The writer of Hebrews says, "God is treating you as sons. For what son is there whom his father does not discipline? If you are left without discipline, in which all have participated, then you are illegitimate children and not sons" (Hebrews 12:7–8). Discipline is simply applying biblical truth in love for the good of the straying family member.

Jesus Relates as Family

Jesus introduces a new definition of family among his disciples. He asks, "'Who is my mother, and who are my brothers?' And stretching out his hand toward his disciples, he said, 'Here are my mother and my brothers! For whoever does the will of my Father in heaven is my brother and sister and mother'" (Matthew 12:48–50). The spiritual family *is* family, according to Jesus. You are *my* brother and *my* sister and *my* mother. One author observes, "Our membership in this spiritual family is an essential part of our Christ-purchased identity and an important fulfillment of God's family promises to his old-covenant people."[3]

Jesus interacts with his disciples with patient perseverance. Most often, they do not quickly understand what he is telling them. For instance, the disciples argue which one of them would be the greatest in the kingdom (Mark 9:33–37). Sadly, leaders in the church still fight for dominance and attention. On another occasion, the disciples mistakenly consider children an annoying distraction, which is contrary to how Jesus views them (Mark 10:13–16). Even Peter denies the Lord before his crucifixion. After his resurrection, Jesus appears to the disciples, addressing them endearingly as children, and has a meal with them (John 21:5 ff.). Then Jesus recommissions Peter, a three-time denier of Jesus, to feed the people as a shepherd of God's flock (John 21:15–17; 1 Peter 5:1–4). Time and again, Jesus exercises patience with the disciples, a skill required of all parents toward their children. Loving, gentle, patient persistence is how Jesus leads the disciples, and how every leader in the church ought to lead. Jesus repeatedly interacts with his disciples less like a group of followers or students and more like a family.[4]

Jesus teaches the disciples to pray to God the Father as "our Father in heaven" (Matthew 6:9). Jesus alone had the right to address God with this kind of filial language, writes R. C. Sproul, "yet he instructed his followers to do the same."[5] They were not to pray to an elusive tyrannical master, but to their Father, who has adopted them as his beloved children (Ephesians 1:4–5). The familial relationship dominates the tone for how we lead the family of God.

Paul Leads as a Father and Brother

Paul refers to Timothy, Titus, and Silas with family terms. He calls Timothy his beloved child that he longs to see so that joy may fill him (2 Timothy 1:2–4). He calls Titus his "true child in a common faith" and then entrusts important ministry to him (Titus 1:4–5). Paul calls Silas (also known as Silvanus) a "faithful brother" (1 Peter 5:12). The familial relationship, rather than apostolic authority, is the basis Paul gives the leaders in Thessalonica to lead the church.

> But we [church leaders] were gentle among you, *like a nursing mother* taking care of her own children. So, being affectionately desirous of you, we were

ready to share with you not only the gospel of God but also our own selves, because you had become very dear to us. . . . For you know how, *like a father with his children*, we exhorted each one of you and encouraged you and charged you to walk in a manner worthy of God, who calls you into his own kingdom and glory. (1 Thessalonians 2:7–8, 11–12)

We must apply this same relationship as we guide others. Paul doesn't just say "mother," but a "nursing mother"—conveying the idea of giving of one's self. Leadership requires that we expend ourselves for others with joy. Similarly, like a father, a leader brings instruction, encouragement, healthy accountability, and discipline when necessary to walk in a manner that glorifies God and "yields the peaceful fruit of righteousness" (Hebrews 12:11). Commenting on Galatians 4:12, Martin Luther argues that by "[Paul's] own example, he admonishes all pastors and ministers to have a fatherly and motherly affection, not toward ravening wolves, but toward the straying sheep. They should bear with their faults and weaknesses, instructing and restoring them with the spirit of meekness, for they cannot be brought back to the right path by any other means."[6] If we know how to lead our families, we know how to lead the church, the family of God (1 Timothy 3:4–5).

We Lead as God's Children

Leaders are not just fathers or mothers in the faith, but children of God. David is not only a shepherd but also a sheep (Psalm 23). The apostle John gives us some insight into the kind of relationship necessary to lead as a child of God rather than as a child of the devil: "See what kind of love the Father has given to us, that we should be called children of God; and so we are. . . . By this it is evident who are the children of God and who are children of the devil" (1 John 3:1a, 10a). The characteristics of children of God are compared with characteristics of children of the Devil in the following list:

Children of God (1 John 3:1, 10)	Children of the Devil (1 John 3:10)
Truth-tellers (John 14:6)	Liars (John 8:44)
Transparent (John 3:19–20; 1 John 1:7–9)	Deceivers (2 Corinthians 11:3, 14; Revelation 12:9)
Embrace others as a family (1 John 3:1–2, 10)	Destroy others as a foe (John 10:10; 1 Peter 5:8)
Advocate for others (1 John 2:1–2)	Accuse others (Zechariah 3:1; Revelation 12:10)
Love selflessly (1 John 3:11, 14)	Selfish (1 John 3:10–12)
Righteous (1 John 3:7)	Rebellious (1 John 3:4, 8)
Sacrifice for others (1 John 3:16)	Withhold from others (1 John 3:17)

On which side of the list are your church leaders? How could you lead as a child of God?

Time to Break the Cycle

I described this manner of familial leadership to a sixty-year-old woman who had been in church all of her life. She said she had never experienced this. That was heartbreaking, but I'm afraid she is not alone. It should not be odd to lead a church like a family. Rather, it should be alarming to run it like a secular organization.

I have been on the receiving end of a church leader's lie, which produced devastating results. It almost ruined me. It tainted my character as a minister. I never retaliated, and I never talked about it to anyone except with a counselor and my closest friends, who helped me process my decimated emotions and residual trauma. Four years later, the church leader who lied about me confessed it to me and asked for forgiveness. The damage, however, was irreversible, and it was traumatic for me and my wife and sons. I granted forgiveness to him, but I asked him why he lied. He says he was trying to protect his reputation. That's not what a father would do to his son or daughter. A godly father sacrifices *his* life for the good of the family. He does not sacrifice another family member for his own benefit. Paul tells the church at Philippi, "Do nothing from selfish ambition or conceit, but in humility count others more significant than yourselves. Let each of you look not only to his own interests, but also to the interests of others" (Philippians 2:3–4).

How could church leaders biblically handle stressful situations like the firing of the staff member mentioned in the opening paragraph? If we have to make changes in how a person serves in the church, we can do it as a mother or father would to an adult son or daughter. That's what a good parent would do and is what a good leader would do. In love, bring the challenge into the light. Discuss the issue to determine if there is any misunderstanding. Collaborate on solutions and next steps. If there appears to be no solution, walk with them in kindness and generosity to be repositioned. Boundaries and discipline implemented are for their benefit, but it doesn't erase our relationship with them. It instead increases our relationship and interactions with them. The erasure of a person is the most extreme form of hatred. At all costs, seek to reconcile broken relationships with humility and urgency (Matthew 5:23–24, 18:15; Romans 12:18).

The church needs to set a countercultural example for how to guide others entrusted to her care. It's time to remove unrepentant bullies from pastoral positions and from the church boardrooms. Paul succinctly gives us critical insight: "Love one another with brotherly affection. Outdo one another in showing honor" (Romans 12:10). Relationships always require correcting, rebuking, and encouraging—with great patience and careful instruction (2 Timothy 4:2). The best way to lead is like a loving father, mother, sister, or brother guiding others toward the heavenly Father.

Your Turn . . .

Prayer for Relating as Family

Lord, the church is a family to love, guide, admonish, and encourage. Help me to regard those in the family as mothers, fathers, sisters, and brothers—all children of God. Let my leadership be characterized by humility, gentleness, patience, love, unity, and peacemaking. Thank you for adopting me into your family through the finished work of Christ. Thank you for leaders of the family who are looking out for my best interest, including my holiness. I don't always act as your child, but you always approach me as my Father.

Coaching Questions:

1. Ministries have to make hard decisions about expenses. If necessary, how would you like to be furloughed in a familial manner?

2. What are the practical ways that you can treat members as sons and daughters?
3. Review the contrast between children of God and children of the Devil. Which side of the list (page 139) have you experienced from leaders?
4. What is the first step you can take toward guiding the church as the family of God?

12.
COACH

Gospel-Shaped Leaders Develop Other Leaders

One coach will impact more young people in one year than
the average person does in a lifetime.

Billy Graham

I had a discussion with a mature pastor with a lot of ability and charisma. He told me that he was going to plant a church in a major city. I asked him if he had considered coaching a young pastor to be the church planter instead of planting it himself. He couldn't comprehend what I was posing. I asked what difference it would make if he trained, coached, encouraged, and equipped a much younger pastor to plant it. "Yes, he can help me," he told me. "But," I inquired, "what if you helped *him* instead?" He stared blankly for a moment and then quietly uttered, "But I could do a better job." This is a prevailing barrier to leadership development.

Faithful Christians will make disciples, but gospel-shaped leaders also focus on making other leaders. A person doesn't learn to lead by attending a class or reading a book on leadership. People best learn to lead when they lead while receiving helpful, honest feedback. I spent thirty-five years as a basketball player and then spent twenty years as a basketball coach at various levels. I painfully accepted that it was not appropriate for me, as the coach, to trot onto the court and start running the offense. A forty-year-old coach can't replace their seventeen-year-old point guard even if they could be more productive than them. My job as a coach was not to play but—and this is significant—to continually and intentionally develop the players entrusted to me so they could play the game at their highest possible level. I had to stay on the sidelines and give direction, guidance, and encouragement. The players had to execute—even if they couldn't do it as well as I could (or as I imagined that I still could). Likewise, spiritually mature leaders always intentionally develop other leaders.

Relational management requires developing other people to build up the ministries (Ephesians 4:11, 16). It takes emotional intelligence to train and equip others to minister. But this process builds the church beyond our abilities.

Six Building Blocks for Developing Others

Jesus calls some fishermen to follow him and be his disciples: "'Come, follow me,' Jesus said, 'and I will send you out to fish for people'" (Matthew 4:19 NIV). They were fishermen when he met them but he developed them to lead in his mission. Jesus took time and made a commitment to the underdeveloped disciples. He taught and modeled with patience, intimacy, persistence, care, and intentionality. He gave them a vision for God's harvest (Matthew 9:36–38), and he sent them with his authority (Matthew 10:5–16; 28:18–20).

Leaders in Christ's mission will recruit, train, build, equip, send, and debrief people to become leaders. Developing potential leaders must be a top priority for the church. When we instruct people to lead, the gospel expands in ways we could never do on our own (Matthew 11:1).

1. *The first building block to develop leaders is to pray for God to send them.* Jesus says the harvest is plentiful but the laborers are few. He instructs leaders to pray to the Lord to send laborers (Matthew 9:37–38; Luke 10:2). We can't hang our heads in desperate need of more leaders if we don't bend our knees to request God's help.

2. *The second building block is to define a leader for your ministry.* We are looking for Christlike, humble servants with a teachable spirit. We need those who love the church's mission and can lead with compassion and gentleness.

3. *The third block is to recruit for specific roles and responsibilities.* My first ministry opportunity came at age nineteen when the youth pastor asked me to use my influence to invite teenagers to church. That was my responsibility and, as a result, my passion to evangelize students grew. I might not have developed if he had only made a general request for me to help with the youth group.

4. *The fourth block is to model leadership.* Paul says, "Be imitators of me as I am of Christ" (1 Corinthians 11:1). He told others, "What you have learned and received and heard and seen in me—practice these things" (Philippians 4:9). Church leadership is a beautiful process of training people to become leaders who develop others (2 Timothy 2:2). It is not automatic. It must become a deliberate activity of every leader in the church.

5. *The fifth building block is to empower, evaluate, and coach the person.* Jesus sent out his disciples with his authority and power to preach and heal (Luke 9:1–6; 10:1, 9). Jesus met with the disciples after they returned from their preaching

and healing ministry. Afterward, he evaluated what took place and he corrected them and coached them (Luke 10:17–20). We cannot expect others to fully develop without coaching.

6. *The sixth block is to be available to develop leaders.* Jesus literally sits down with his disciples to teach them (Matthew 5:1; Mark 9:35; John 6:3; 8:2). He is present and accessible. We cannot be too busy to develop others. I have several young men who call me many times a month. They are learning to lead, and I am happy they feel that I am accessible. It costs me time and energy, but it is my top ministry priority.

To develop others, we have to be in a significant relationship with them. We have to care enough about them and their experiences to listen, love, and guide them. To develop others, we cannot be self-absorbed. We either empty ourselves daily, or we will become full of ourselves. If we focus on our own aspirations and interests, we will never develop others. Gospel-shaped leaders place the needs of others above their own needs. We are servants first and leaders second.[1]

Throw in the Towel: What It Means to Develop Others

Toward the end of Jesus's life, at a feast with his disciples, Jesus demonstrates the heart of a leader. Removing his outer garment and tying a towel around his waist, he kneels down and washes the disciples' feet. He then puts back on his outer garment and sits with them to explain what he has done: "You call me Teacher and Lord, and you are right, for so I am. If I then, your Lord and Teacher, have washed your feet, you also ought to wash one another's feet. For I have given you an example, that you also should do just as I have done to you" (John 13:13–15).

What does it mean to develop others? First, we remove the outer garment of earthly identity. Jesus, the Teacher, wore an outer garment, but he removed it. Gospel-shaped leaders strive to discard their titles and positions and any self-aggrandizing status if it gets in the way of serving others. Church leaders must not hide behind jobs, net worth, education, position, age, or achievement. They remove the outer garment that may lead to pride, and they eagerly take on a servant's towel.

Second, gospel-shaped leaders develop people by serving them with joy. This kind of leader does what is best for others without getting any praise or recognition. We have to guard our motivations and hearts continually. The act of Jesus washing feet is undignified. Perhaps that's why Peter initially refuses this act of servanthood by Jesus. He knows Jesus is above this demeaning activity. But Jesus knows he is not at all above it. He submits to being hung on a cross as an extension of this selfless act of service for others. Jesus does not need a Savior. He isn't the benefactor; he is a servant who sacrifices for the good of others. Severian, Bishop of Gabala in Syria, said of Jesus in AD 400, "He who wraps the heavens in clouds wrapped round himself a towel. He who pours the water into the rivers and pools tipped . . . water into a basin. And he before whom every knee bends in heaven and on earth and under the earth knelt to wash the feet of his disciples."[2]

Third, gospel-shaped leaders demonstrate the attitude necessary to develop others. Jesus says his act of servanthood is an example for us to follow: "A servant is not greater than his master, nor is a messenger greater than the one who sent him" (John 13:15–16). If we follow Jesus, we must also serve others. If leaders want to lead others into an activity or attitude, they often need to demonstrate it to others. Jesus says in essence, "If I, your leader, am willing to serve others and not be the recipient of honor, you must be willing to serve others in the same way."

Thomas à Kempis wrote, "Jesus hath many lovers of His heavenly kingdom, but few bearers of His Cross."[3] We must view ourselves as servants on a battleship and not as consumers on a cruise ship. A leader has to be willing to do the less prestigious tasks like hoisting the sails, mopping the deck, bailing water, or peeling the potatoes. No matter our level of education, experience, or giftedness, we must be willing to do what is best for the vessel's mission. When we put ourselves above serving others, our leadership will begin eroding, and a mutiny will most likely emerge.

Immature leaders are like the young Joseph in Genesis 37, who flaunted the coat of many colors given to him by his father. We may secretly want to wear the colorful robe and have people bow down to us. Maturing as a leader takes adversity, accepting responsibility for our actions, and, most of all, understanding the importance of developing others. God put Joseph in power, and in a position of authority over his brothers not so that his brothers would bow down to him, but so that Joseph could serve God by providing for his people.

Developing people requires an honest evaluation of their strengths and weaknesses related to the task at hand. For instance, one older man asked me, as his pastor, if he could hand out bulletins at the church door. He was eager to serve. The problem was that he wasn't aware that his demeanor was not welcoming at all. He had a surly attitude and a grouchy look on his face, and we knew he could be helpful elsewhere, just not as a greeter. Just because someone is excited about something doesn't mean that they are any good at it. One writer reminds us of using people where they are most gifted: "Never try to teach a pig to sing; it wastes your time and annoys the pig."[4] We redirected the man to join the finance team since most of them are already grumpy anyway. (I'm kidding—kind of.) He became the church treasurer. Redirecting others is not being judgmental or critical. Rather it helps others identify where they can contribute and, thus, have the most spiritually fulfilling experience.

We have to learn to assess people's strengths and weaknesses and then serve them by asking them to consider the activity where they best fit within the team's context. Leaders must be the first to remove their outer cloak, take the towel, kneel before others, and wash the feet of those they lead. It's what Jesus did.

Your Turn . . .

Prayer for Developing Other Leaders

Lord, you have entrusted people to our care to be equipped so they can strengthen the body. To produce much fruit, we must die to our desires and align with yours. Help me to empty myself and be a servant. Use me to accomplish *your* will among *your* people. Help me to kneel down and serve others, taking the lowest job if necessary, without any regard to recognition.

Coaching Questions

1. Who are some people that you can intentionally develop?

2. What fears or reluctance do you have about intentionally developing other leaders?
3. On which of the six building blocks for developing others (pages 145–146) do you need to focus your attention?
4. What attitudes or practices do you need to change to develop leaders in your context?

13.
YOKE

Gospel-Shaped Leaders Pursue
Meaningful Friendships

Friendship is a deep oneness that develops as two people,
speaking the truth in love to each other, journey together
to the same horizon. Spiritual friendship is the greatest
journey of all, because the horizon is so high and far, yet
sure—it is the "day of Jesus Christ" and what we will be
like when we finally see him face-to-face.[1]

Timothy Keller

C hurch leaders are real people with real problems but often
few real friends. I don't know why that is, but it seems to
be consistent among Christian leaders. Some have had friends
burn them and trust is now difficult. I had leaders betray me
and it's a barrier in my subconscious mind. I sometimes think
not having a friend is less painful than having a friend who
may betray me. But I need friends who I can trust. One of my
best friends in ministry misused a conversation between us as
ammunition for another leader to attack me. It still hurts. But
I know if I fail to unite with a close community of believers, I
am vulnerable to an all-out demonic siege. Leaders who stand
alone are exposed to the attacks of Satan and his bloodthirsty
legion of demons: "Be sober-minded; be watchful. Your ad-
versary the devil prowls around like a roaring lion, seeking

someone to devour" (1 Peter 5:8). I need other people for my endurance in ministry. Others need me for theirs.

One study disclosed that at least 70 percent of pastors in the United States claim they have no friends.[2] That is an alarming statistic. Some believe that church leaders should not pursue friendships with those in their church. They may be afraid to have friendships, especially if others have burned them in the past. A lack of meaningful relationships leads to loneliness and may lead to moral failure, burnout, or depression.

Yoke Together with Friends

The biblical warning to not yoke with unbelievers is most commonly applied to dating, even though the passage is not directly about dating or marriage (2 Corinthians 6:14). The Corinthian believers became emotionally entangled with someone or something that dampened their affection for Christ.

Christ implores us, "Take my yoke upon you, and learn from me, for I am gentle and lowly in heart, and you will find rest for your souls. For my yoke is easy, and my burden is light" (Matthew 11:29–30). In farming, a yoke is a wooden crosspiece typically fastened over the necks of two animals and attached to the plow or cart they are to pull. Christ invites us to connect with him to accomplish his purposes for our lives. But he doesn't add weight upon our necks; he makes it light. Likewise, we need Christlike friends to yoke together to accomplish Christ's calling. We cannot fight the good fight of faith alone for prolonged periods. We need others to help bear the load of ministry.

We need to unite under a divine oath, and perseveringly stand side by side with other believers (Philippians 1:27). We need to fight for one another with every weapon in our arsenal. We often face problems in the church because we are so busy fighting *with* each other that we fail to fight *for* each other. Amid the confusion, destruction, and the threat of enemy attack, Nehemiah says, "Do not be afraid of them. Remember the Lord, who is great and awesome, and fight for your brothers, your sons, your daughters, your wives, and your homes" (Nehemiah 4:14).

Know Your Enemy: Seven Strategies of Satan

Before we can fight for one another, we need to obtain information about our enemy's tactics. We must defend against seven common strategies of demonic warfare:

1. **Doubt.** An attack on a rogue believer generally begins with uncertainty over the authority and reliability of God's Word: "Did God actually say?" (Genesis 3:1). Without others around us to challenge our unbelief, we fall quickly into relying on our own wisdom.
2. **Diversion.** Without a troop of friends fighting alongside, a lone soldier often turns aside from the primary mission and foundation of the faith to focus on secondary and tertiary issues instead of the doctrines of first importance (1 Corinthians 15:3).
3. **Deception.** A believer lacking real friendships in the local church is susceptible to the schemes of Satan, who is the father of lies (John 8:44). Deception tricks us into believing that the proverbial Trojan horse is harmless, so we open the door to attacking forces.

4. **Division.** Jesus prays for the unity of believers (John 17). Jesus wants Christians to completely give themselves to one another in community, just as the Father, Son, and Spirit enjoy real community.

5. **Disruption.** Disruption occurs when others question the leader's character, and mutinous gossip persists without concern for unity. Submission to Christ as the head of the church is crucial for a believer's effective defense against demonic craftiness.

6. **Dominance.** A believer, living outside the protection of a community, is swarmed under massive spiritual, emotional, and psychological attacks.

7. **Destruction.** Devastation overcomes believers in many ways. Jesus says, "Every kingdom divided against itself is laid waste, and a divided household falls" (Luke 11:17). Sin, when fully grown, results in death (James 1:15). The end goal of Satan is the destruction of Christian leaders. When Satan destroys leaders, their disciples fall away.

Gospel Friendship

Church leaders must shepherd those in their charge to be strong in the Lord and in the strength of his might. We must help them to depend on the armor of God to be able to stand against the devil's schemes (Ephesians 6:10–11). God entrusts shepherds to lead and care for the souls of his flock. While the instruction in the following passage is primarily for elders, we can extend the application to all believers, who should exercise spiritual care for others as gospel friends: "Shepherd the flock of God that is among you, exercising oversight, not under compulsion, but willingly, as God would have you; not for shameful gain, but eagerly; not domineering over those in your charge, but being examples to the flock (1 Peter 5:2–3).

In these verses, the apostle Peter identifies four critical characteristics of gospel friendship that are necessary as we fight for one another:

1. Gospel friends initiate a reproducible example as an image-bearer of Jesus. Be an example, Peter writes (1 Peter 5:3). Jesus provides a pattern for his disciples to follow. He does not control their actions. He models worshipful obedience to God. Leaders are undershepherds—submissive agents of Jesus, the chief Shepherd. Making disciples is the church's mission, and it includes displaying God to unbelieving neighbors, relatives, and friends. Our friendships with others are important examples for others to follow.

2. Gospel friends initiate relationships with the people near them. "Shepherd the flock of God that is among you," Peter writes (1 Peter 5:2). God has placed us in relationships where we can care for those around us. We do not have to look for others to befriend. They are all around us: homes, neighborhoods, offices, classrooms, and churches. People tend to escape or wander into isolation. A sheep left alone will starve, fall into the jaws of wolves, or wander into danger. But if a shepherd is present, protection is near. Leaders themselves must be willing to be under the care of another while also shepherding people.

3. Gospel friends initiate relationships despite their needs. God's glory motivates this interaction. "As a fellow elder and a witness of the sufferings of Christ, as well as a partaker in the glory that is going to be revealed" (1 Peter 5:1). Authentic gospel friends are first believers who recognize that they are laboring for the King alongside others who are likewise in need. They are simultaneously a shepherd and a sheep. Often, we have to fight as wounded soldiers because the mission and the defense of others' lives demand it. Friendship is rarely convenient.

4. Gospel friends initiate caring acts of service for others. "Not under compulsion, but willingly," Peter writes (1 Peter 5:2). Jesus talks about the shepherd who abandons the sheep when trouble arises (John 10:12–13). In our self-centered society, we often discard people in our lives without much thought. If someone isn't forcing us to care for them or if we do not think we are responsible for them, we do not shepherd them through their difficulties because it costs too much. Gospel friendship isn't flippant about relationships.

Gospel friendship in the church displays Jesus's love for us and authenticates our friendship with him (John 15:15). When we love one another, we commit to care for others even as we are cared for by others. We must take this gospel-friendship oath seriously, initiating a real community with those God yokes together with us to fight for God's glory.

Three Types of Friendships

Ministry leaders have three types of friendships: (1) mentee friendships where we invest time for the advancement of other people, (2) mentor friendships where we are the recipients of others pouring into us, and (3) mutual friendships. I have often had mostly mentee-type friendships. The problem with these kinds of friendships is that when circumstances change, the friendship often ends abruptly. When you experience a need, mentees will not generally feel compelled toward a mutual friendship.

Both mentor and mentee relationships drain us. This spent energy is not a bad thing, but it can't be the only kind of friendship we experience. Mutual friendships benefit both parties. These are the kinds of relationships we want to develop, in which we "exhort one another every day, as long as it is called 'today,' that none of you may be hardened by the deceitfulness of sin" (Hebrews 3:13). Dane Ortlund remarks about friendship, "Mutuality is a two-way relationship of joy, comfort, and openness, that of peers, as distinct from a one-way relationship, such as that of a king to subject or parent to child."[3] Richard Sibbes describes friendship as mutual consent, mutual sympathy, mutual solace, and mutual honor and respect for one another.[4] Without mutual friendships, our soul will thirst for life-giving companionship and will wilt in despair if not met.

Pursue Mutual Friendships

We need friends who love us sacrificially and unconditionally; friends we can trust and with whom we can find joy. These kinds of friendships are rare, but not impossible. J. C. Ryle wrote, "This world is full of sorrow because it is full of sin. It is a dark place. It is a lonely place. It is a disappointing place. The brightest sunbeam in it is a friend. Friendship halves our sorrows and doubles our joys."[5]

Jesus's resurrection has broken down the middle wall of partition with God and others (Ephesians 2:13–22). Through Christ's incarnation, we are no longer called servants, but friends (Luke 12:4; John 15:15). As we pursue Jesus as our friend and yokemate, we can likewise pursue gospel friendships to yoke together to glorify God. Proverbs tells us, "A man of many companions may come to ruin, but there is a friend who sticks closer than a brother" (Proverbs 18:24). That friend is certainly Jesus, but you can be that gospel friend for others, and they can be that friend for you. I need the gospel application that my friend brings into my life, and my friend needs the gospel application that I can bring into their life. Dietrich Bonhoeffer said in *Life Together*, "The Christ in [our] own heart is weaker than the Christ in the word of [our] brother [and sister]; [our] own heart is uncertain, [our] brother's [and sister's] is sure. And that also clarifies the goal of all Christian community: they meet one another as bringers of the message of salvation."[6]

Friendship with Jesus is unbreakable because he will never fail you, reject you, neglect you, or betray you. He looks compassionately into our insecure souls and makes an offer of true friendship, "Take my yoke upon you, and learn from me, for I am gentle and lowly in heart, and you will find rest for your souls. For my yoke is easy, and my burden is light" (Matthew 11:29–30).

Yoke first with Jesus and then yoke with real friends who will, with Jesus, lighten your burdens in life. Gospel-shaped leaders pursue others in a Christlike relationship, and they allow others to pursue them. We were not made by God to walk this journey alone. "Whoever isolates himself seeks his own desire; he breaks out against all sound judgment" (Proverbs 18:1). Yoked with Christ and real friends, our spiritual and emotional health will flourish to enable us to lean on Jesus to shepherd his people.

You and your friends can start a revolution of gospel-shaped leaders who lead the church in a God-glorifying way. The current model may not be working, but the gospel has given us a glorious template to follow so we can lean on Jesus to shepherd his people.

Your Turn . . .

Prayer for Friendships

Lord, you sent your Son, Jesus, to befriend us and to be our yokemate. We need others who will partner with us to defeat the enemy. Provide bringers of the gospel in our lives to encourage us, challenge us, and support us as we strive side by side for the advancement of the gospel. Help us to be aware of the strategies of the enemy and provide those who will fight with us to overthrow demonic forces. Help us to be a friend to others in the ministry you have chosen for us.

Coaching Questions

1. What are the characteristics of a true friend?
2. What would it look like to have one or two real friends in your life?
3. How can your friendship with Jesus inform your friendships with others?
4. What broken relationship needs reconciling and how will you pursue it?

Conclusion

Where Are the Gospel-Shaped Leaders?

Where are the gospel-shaped leaders who will answer the call to lead the Lord's work in the Lord's way? The church needs leaders who will mirror the gospel in their leadership, not just their words. The body of Christ needs men and women who will enliven believers to rejoice in the good news of Jesus.

The church needs leaders who do not think they are a big deal. We need those who die to self so others can thrive. We need humble leaders willing to serve unnoticed. We need those who will walk with the Father and invite others along.

The church needs leaders who believe holiness is not old-fashioned. It's a biblical requirement for church leaders. We need leaders who will savor the living words of Jesus and repent daily.

The church needs those who love her as Christ loves his bride. It doesn't need leaders who serve their own interests. We need people who will radiate the gospel by speaking to others with grace, leading in love and gentleness.

The church needs leaders who will work with others to attempt God-sized goals. We need people who will inspire others in their faith. We need those who will heal broken relationships and be peacemakers.

We need leaders who will pray knowing that everything depends on God. We need those who dig deep into God's Word and crave it for their second-by-second nourishment. We need people who have an utter reliance on the power of the Spirit to accomplish God's will.

Where are the gospel-shaped leaders who will lean on Jesus to shepherd his people? Now is the time for a change in the way we lead the church.

Will you answer that call to be a gospel-shaped leader today?

"So guard yourselves and God's people. Feed and shepherd God's flock—his church, purchased with his own blood—over which the Holy Spirit has appointed you as leaders" (Acts 20:28 NLT).

Endnotes

Chapter 1

1. William Tyndale, "A Pathway into the Holy Scripture," included in his *Doctrinal Treatises and Introductions to Different Portions of the Holy Scriptures*, ed. The Parker Society (Cambridge: CYP, 1848), 8–9.

2. Charles H. Spurgeon, *Lectures to My Students*, Vol. 1 (Albany, OR: AGES Digital Library) 12, 22.

3. Daniel Goleman, *What Makes a Leader?* (Boston, MA: Harvard Business School Publishing Corporation, 2017), 1.

4. Goleman, *What Makes a Leader?*, 7.

5. Valerie Strauss, The Surprising Thing Google Learned about Its Employees and What It Means for Today's Students," *Washington Post*, December 20, 2017, https://www.washingtonpost.com/news/answer-sheet/wp/2017/12/20/the-surprising-thing-google-learned-about-its-employees-and-what-it-means-for-todays-students/.

Chapter 2

1. C. S. Lewis, *Mere Christianity* (New York: Macmillan, 1952), 154.

2. *Braveheart*, directed by Mel Gibson (Hollywood, CA: Paramount, 1995).

3. "NP View: Once Again a Man Dies So That Others Can Be Saved," *National Post* (Toronto), March 30, 2018, http://nationalpost.com/opinion/np-view-once-again-a-man-dies-so-that-others-can-be-saved.

4. Seth Godin, *What to Do When It's Your Turn* (New York: The Domino Project, 2014), 8.

Chapter 3

1. John Calvin, *Institutes of the Christian Religion*, ed. John T. McNeill, vol. 1 (Louisville, KY: Westminster John Knox Press, 2006), 612.

Chapter 4

1. Scott Thomas and Tom Wood, *Gospel Coach: Shepherding Leaders to Glorify God* (Grand Rapids, MI: Zondervan, 2012).
2. Richard Ellsworth Day, *Bush Aglow: The Life Story of D. L. Moody* (Philadelphia, PA: Judson Press, 1936), 275.
3. Martin Luther King Jr., "What Is Your Life's Blueprint?" Filmed 1967 in Philadelphia, https://www.youtube.com/watch?v=kmsAxX84cjQ&feature=emb_logo.
4. *The Works of Jonathan Edwards*, Vol. 1 (Edinburgh: 1995), loc. 77788, Kindle.
5. Gilbert Harman, "Moral Philosophy Meets Social Psychology: Virtue Ethics and the Fundamental Attribution Error," *Proceedings of the Aristotelian Society*, New Series, 99 (1999): 315–31, www.jstor.org/stable/4545312.
6. Private message used by permission.
7. Mo Pitney, "Take the Chance," *Behind This Guitar* (Curb Records, 2016).
8. My Child at Cerebral Palsy.org. "Jerry Traylor: Athlete Proves That Success Is a Worthwhile Climb," accessed November 30, 2020, https://www.cerebralpalsy.org/inspiration/athletes/jerry-traylor.
9. Seth A. Rosenthal and Todd L. Pittinsky, "Narcissistic Leadership," *The Leadership Quarterly* 17, no. 6 (2006): 617–33, https://doi.org/10.1016/j.leaqua.2006.10.005.

Chapter 5

1. J. C. Ryle, *A Call to Prayer* (Carlisle, PA: Banner of Truth, 2002), 16.
2. Ray Ortlund (@rayortlund), "Jesus isn't impressed with our reputations." Twitter, February 26, 2019, 3:17 p.m., https://twitter.com/rayortlund/status/1100490076042203137.
3. Franklin Graham, *Billy Graham in Quotes* (Nashville, TN: Thomas Nelson, 2011), 105.

4. Andrew Bonar, *Memoir and Remains of the Rev. Robert Murray McCheyne* (Edinburgh: Banner of Truth, 1894), 293.

5. Paul David Tripp, "Speaking Redemptively," *Journal of Biblical Counseling* 16, no. 3, (1998): 10–18, https://rhemacounseling.com/wp-content/uploads/2016/04/1603010-Speaking-Redemptively.pdf.

6. John Stott, *The Message of 2 Timothy* (Downers Grove, IL: IVP, 1973), 76.

Chapter 6

1. Kenneth P. De Meuse, Guangrong Dai, George Hallenbeck, "Learning agility: A construct whose time has come," *Consulting Psychology Journal: Practice and Research*, 62(2) (June 2010): 120, https://doi.org/10.1037/a0019988.

2. Bill Joiner and Stephen Josephs, *Leadership Agility: Five Levels of Mastery for Anticipating and Initiating Change* (San Francisco, CA: Jossey-Bass, 2007), v.

3. "A New Chapter," Trinity Grace Church (website), 2018, http://www.trinitygracechurch.com.

4. Personal Interview with Mark Reynolds, July 20, 2020.

5. Tommy Wells, "Restaurant Gets Inventive to Attract Customers," *Eastland County Today*, April 16, 2020, https://newzgroup.com/TXLegals/2020/96815-2020-04-16_1002.pdf.

6. Karen Arnold, *Lives of Promise: What Becomes of High School Valedictorians: A Fourteen-year Study of Achievement and Life Choices* (San Francisco, CA: Jossey Bass, 1995).

7. Eric Barker, *Barking Up the Wrong Tree* (New York, NY: HarperOne Publishing, 2017), 9–10.

8. Ray Ortlund, *The Gospel: How the Church Portrays the Beauty of Christ* (Wheaton, IL: Crossway Books, 2014), 15–20.

9. Warren Bennis and Robert J. Thomas, "Crucibles of Leadership," *Harvard Business Review*, September 2002, https://hbr.org/2002/09/crucibles-of-leadership.

10. Donald Whitney, "The Discipline of Learning," *Tabletalk Magazine*, November 1, 2011, https://www.ligonier.org/learn/articles/the-discipline-of-learning/.

11. Richard Ellsworth Day, *Bush Aglow: The Life Story of D. L. Moody* (Philadelphia, PA: Judson Press, 1936), 272.

12. R. C. Sproul, "Renewing Your Mind," https://www.ligonier.org/learn/devotionals/renewing-your-mind/.

Chapter 7

1. Charles H. Spurgeon, *Lectures to My Students, Vol. 1 (Albany, OR: AGES Digital Library),* 175.

2. R. C. Sproul, "Sabbath Rest" in *Themes from Genesis* (n.d.). Retrieved February 08, 2021, https://www.ligonier.org/learn/media/sabbath-rest/.

3. Paul David Tripp, *Dangerous Calling: The Unique Challenges of Pastoral Ministry* (Wheaton, IL: Crossway, 2012), 105.

4. Bruce K. Waltke and Cathi J. Fredricks, *Genesis: A Commentary* (Grand Rapids, MI: Zondervan, 2001), 71–72.

5. Matthew Sleeth, *24/6: A Prescription for a Healthier, Happier Life* (Carol Stream, IL: Tyndale, 2012), 25.

6. Peter Scazzero, *Emotionally Healthy Spirituality* (Nashville: Thomas Nelson, 2006), 171.

7. Spurgeon, *Lectures*, 175.

8. We do not have to be a Sabbatarian to practice a Sabbath. Sabbatarians believe the observance of the Sabbath is a continuing obligation for the Christian. See David Strain, "Why Christians Should Be Sabbatarians," October 27, 2020, https://www.thegospelcoalition.org/article/christians-sabbatarians/ for a helpful understanding.

9. Sleeth, *24/6*, 6–7.

10. Archibald D. Hart, *The Anxiety Cure: You Can Find Emotional Tranquility and Wholeness* (Nashville, TN: Word Publishing, 1999), 150.

11. Jeff Behar, "Rest and Overtraining: What Does This Mean to Bodybuilders?" November 14, 2018, http://www.bodybuilding.com/fun/behar2.htm.

12. Spurgeon, *Lectures*, 179.

13. Archibald D. Hart, "Depressed, Stressed, and Burned Out: What's Going on in My Life?" *Enrichment* 11, no. 3 (Summer 2006): 21.

14. Spurgeon, *Lectures*, 173.

15. Hart, "Depressed, Stressed, and Burned Out," 22.

16. John Piper, "Remember the Sabbath Day to Keep It Holy," Desiring God, October 6, 1985, https://www.desiringgod.org/messages/remember-the-sabbath-day-to-keep-it-holy.

17. Terry Hershey, *Sacred Necessities: Gifts for Living with Passion, Purpose, and Grace* (Notre Dame, IN: Ave Maria Press, 2005), 68–69.

18. John Calvin, *Commentary upon the Acts of the Apostles* Volume 2 (Grand Rapids, MI: Baker Books, 2003), 255.

19. Spurgeon, *Lectures*, 141–42.

Chapter 8

1. *The Works of Saint Augustine: A Translation for the 21ˢᵗ Century, Sermons III* (184-229Z), trans. Edmund Hill (New Rochelle, NY: New City Press, 1993), 145.

2. J. I. Packer, *A Quest for Godliness: The Puritan Vision of the Christian Life* (Wheaton, IL: Crossway Books, 1990), 65.

3. Francis A. Schaeffer, *The Mark of the Christian* (Downers Grove, IL: Intervarsity Press, 1970), 45–55.

4. A. C. Dixon, *Through Night to Morning* (Grand Rapids, MI: Baker Book House, 1969), 61.

5. Lyle W. Dorsett, *A Passion for Souls: The Life of D. L. Moody* (Chicago, IL: Moody, 1997), 139.

6. Samuel E. Waldron, *A Modern Exposition of the 1689 Baptist Confession of Faith* (Durham, England: Evangelical Press, 1999), 307.

7. Robert Peterson and Alexander Strauch, *Agape Leadership: Lessons in Spiritual Leadership from the Life of R. C. Chapman* (Littleton, CO: Lewis and Roth, 1991), 72.

8. Peterson and Strauch, *Agape Leadership*, 21.

Chapter 9

1. C. S. Lewis, *Mere Christianity* (New York: Macmillan, 1952), 94.

2. Mark Dever, *The Message of the Old Testament: Promises Made* (Wheaton IL: Crossway, 2006), 766.

3. Raymond C. Ortlund Jr., *Proverbs: Wisdom That Works* (Wheaton, IL: Crossway, 2012), 165.

Chapter 10

1. Dane Ortlund, "Want to Be Like Jesus? Be Gentle," The Gospel Coalition, October 17, 2018, https://www.thegospelcoalition.org/article/want-jesus-gentle/.

2. Paul David Tripp, "Speaking Redemptively," *Journal of Biblical Counseling* 16, no. 3 (1998): 18, https://rhemacounseling.com/wp-content/uploads/2016/04/1603010-Speaking-Redemptively.pdf.

3. Dietrich Bonhoeffer, *Life Together* (New York: Harper Collins, 1954), 23.

4. Roy T. Bennett (@InspiringThinkn), "One word of encouragement can be enough," Twitter, July 15, 2017, 1:23 a.m., https://twitter.com/InspiringThinkn/status/886093888384925696.

5. John E. Smith, ed., *The Works of Jonathan Edwards*, vol. 2: Religious Affections (New Haven, CT: Yale University Press, 2009).

Chapter 11

1. J. I. Packer, *Knowing God* (Downers Grove, IL: Intervarsity Press, 1993), 206–7.

2. Albert C. Outler, ed., *John Wesley* (Oxford: Oxford University Press, 1964), 49.

3. Megan Hill, *A Place to Belong: Learning to Love the Local Church* (Wheaton, IL: Crossway Books, 2020), 104.

4. Edward L. Smither, *Augustine as Mentor: A Model for Preparing Spiritual Leaders* (Nashville, TN: B&H Academics, 2008), 19.

5. R. C. Sproul, *Truths We Confess: A Systematic Exposition of the Westminster Confession of Faith* (Sanford, FL: Reformation Trust, 2019), 284.

6. Martin Luther, *Galatians* (Wheaton, IL: Crossway, 1998), 218–19.

Chapter 12

1. R. K. Greenleaf, *Servant Leadership* (Mahwah, NJ: Paulist Press, 1977), 21, 30.
2. Frederick Dale Bruner, *The Gospel of John, A Commentary* (Grand Rapids: Eerdmans, 2012), 748.
3. Thomas à Kempis, *The Imitation of Christ*, trans. William Benham (repr., UK: Compass Circle, 2019), 40.
4. Robert Heinlein, *Time Enough for Love: The Lives of Lazarus Long* (New York, NY: Ace Books, G. P. Putnam's Sons, 1973), 31.

Chapter 13

1. Timothy Keller, *The Meaning of Marriage: Facing the Complexities of Commitment with the Wisdom of God* (New York, NY: Penguin Books, 2011), loc. 1470, Kindle.
2. Charles Crismier, "The Significance of Serving." Retrieved February 09, 2021, from http://ministrytodaymag.com/index.php/ministry-outreach/service/830-the-significance-of-serving.
3. Dane Ortlund, *Gentle and Lowly: The Heart of Christ for Sinners and Sufferers* (Wheaton, IL: Crossway, 2020), 118–19.
4. A. Grosart, ed., *The Complete Works of Richard Sibbes,* vol. 2 (Edinburgh: James Nichol, 1862), 37.
5. J. C. Ryle, "The Best Friend," Grace Gems, https://www.gracegems.org/Ryle/best_friend.htm.
6. Dietrich Bonhoeffer, *Life Together: The Classic Exploration of Christian Community* (New York, NY: Harper One, 2009), 23.